Reference Services in Academic Research Libraries

by

Paula D. Watson

Assistant Director of General Services

Head Central Reference Services

University of Illinois Library at Urbana-Champaign

Reference and Adult Services Division

American Library Association

1986

ISBN:  0-8389-7047-8

Foreword

The compilation of the data from this survey was a long process interrupted many times by the pressures of other responsibilities. It was accomplished with the help of many hands. Every effort has been made to assure accuracy, but it seems inevitable that some errors have found their way into the tables. The compiler apologizes in advance for these and would ask that any errors identified be reported so that corrections may be issued.

# CONTENTS

List of Tables, Figures and Summaries

vi

INTRODUCTION

Reported here are the results of a survey of the memberships of two

groups in the Reference and Adult Services Division of the American

Library Association:  the Reference Services in Large Research Libraries

Discussion Group and the Reference Services in Medium-Sized Libraries

Discussion Group.  The primary aim of the survey was to collect

information on the staffing, organization, and functions of reference

departments in academic research libraries.  It is expected that the

data presented here will be of interest not only to heads of reference

departments in the larger university libraries, but also to reference

managers in other types of libraries, to senior library administrators

in a variety of libraries and to working reference librarians.  In

addition to the data compiled here, the survey also requested a wide

variety of policy and administrative documents which have been published

separately.[1]

The survey was conducted under the auspices of the Reference

Services in Large Research Libraries Discussion Group.  A similar study

was done by the same group in 1977[2].  The project reported on here

collected much more detailed data and extended the 1977 sample to

include both "large" and "medium-sized" research libraries.  Since the

sample is arbitrarily limited to the academic memberships of the two ALA

RASD Discussion Groups (as represented by existing mailing lists for

these groups), it includes the reference departments of almost all the academic libraries which are members of the Association of Research Libraries as well as the reference departments of the four largest predominantly black universities (who are members of the Discussion Group on Reference Services in Large Research Libraries.)

A subcommittee of the large research libraries discussion group[3] worked on drafting an appropriate questionnaire. The new instrument was to be based on the one used in the 1977 survey but the Committee attempted refinements to avoid the oversimplifications which made the first questionnaire difficult for some respondents to answer. The number of questions was increased in order to take into account factors which had been identified in the 1977 survey, but not explored, and known changes in the practice of reference librarianship. The completed questionnaire was mailed to the 106 academic members of both discussion groups in May of 1983. The data reported here therefore represent the state of reference services in the libraries surveyed in the academic year 1982/1983. The majority of responses were received in the summer of 1983. A follow-up mailing produced several additional replies, but completed questionnaires continued to trickle in through spring 1984.

Sixty-six reference departments (or 62.3 percent) returned more or less fully completed questionnaires. Since the questionnaire was largely predicated on the existence of a central reference department in the responding library, we anticipated that subject/divisional libraries would not be able to answer most of the questions. A few of the more general questions were therefore designated by asterisks for subject/divisional libraries to answer. Five institutions (4.7 percent) returned the questionnaires with answers to the designated questions. These five were the University of British Columbia; the University of California, Davis; the University of Guelph, the University of North Carolina and Southern Illinois University. Two other libraries (Purdue and Virginia Polytechnic) responded that they were essentially subject/divisional libraries with no centralized reference services and did not return the questionnaire. The percentage of responses which resulted in some useful information about the responding library was therefore about 69 percent. The data presented in this report were compiled from the responses of the sixty-six reference departments which returned completed, or nearly completed questionnaires. The forty non-respondents included all four predominantly black universities who are members of the large research libraries discussion group and five of the eleven Canadian libraries in the sample. The data reported should therefore be reasonably representative of the state of reference services in American libraries of a certain size at the time of the survey year 1982/1983.

# GENERAL REFERENCE SERVICES IN ACADEMIC RESEARCH LIBRARIES

## Staffing of Reference Departments and Services Offered

Since reference departments are frequently the largest public
services units in academic libraries, comparative staff size and
allocation of human resources within departments are potentially
questions of considerable interest to reference managers as well as to
higher-level library administrators.  The questionnaire asked
respondents to supply the number of fulltime equivalent staff in four
categories:  professional librarians, clerical staff, pre-professional
staff and student assistants:  Throughout the questionnaire the term
"clerical" staff is used to denote all staff members assigned to
reference departments who are not on professional or pre-professional
appointments and who are not unspecialized student workers.  Such
individuals may be referred to in their home institutions as support
staff; non-academic staff; library, reference or technical assistants;
or paraprofessionals.  "Pre-professionals" are defined as library school
students who work in reference departments.  Table 1 displays the
staffing figures supplied by the responding libraries.  The number of
fulltime equivalent reference professionals in the responding
departments ranges from a high of 15.75 at the University of Delaware to
a low of 3.0 at Brigham Young University.  The footnotes to Table 1
begin to suggest a picture of the diversity in basic organization and

functions of reference departments which accounts for the wide

variations in staff size from institution to institution. Most of the

respondents answered the questionnaire with reference to the unit of

their library which provides general reference service. As defined by

the respondents general reference service usually includes broad

responsibility for the humanities and social sciences (See also

discussion below of subject areas in which reference service is provided

and Summary 1.) As the notes indicate, at New York University, social

science reference service is provided at a point separate from the

general reference service point and the staffing levels reported on

Table 1 are for two general service desks. For both Brown and Johns Hopkins,

Table 1 figures also reflect staffing to support two service points, in

both cases a separate science reference desk. The broad functions

encompassed by the reference department at the University of Delaware

make it difficult to reasonably compare its staff complement with that

of other, more traditionally organized, reference departments. The

service arrangements at Temple likewise make staff size comparison with

other departments particularly difficult.

As is evident from the data reported on Table 1, there is also a

wide variation in the number of support staff assigned to research

library reference departments. The number allocated varies from a high

of 22.5 at the University of Houston (where reference has very broadly

defined responsibilities) to a low of zero at Case Western and Columbia.

The clerical staff complement for each department is likely to be even

more dependent than the professional staff complement on the number of

what might be termed "peripheral" services which are under the

administration of the department, for example, responsibility for a periodicals or a microforms room.  These variations will be discussed further below.

A few reference departments which are at institutions where there are library schools are able to flesh out their staffs with, presumably highly-motivated but inexperienced, library school students.  Such students may have official appointments, or they may, possibly, be paid as hourly employees.  (For the purpose of calculating the total line staff assigned to the department shown in the next to last column of the Table, they are assumed to have official appointments.)  At the University of Illinois at Urbana-Champaign, for example, the library school students hold graduate-assistantships which are line items in the budget.  Library school students are assumed to be of more value to reference departments than ordinary hourly student workers because of their higher level of interest in the work and their desire to acquire practical experience.  Their usefulness is also increased by the knowledge and skills they acquire during the employment period both through coursework and on-the-job exposure.  Twenty-one reference departments report the employment of pre-professionals.  This is about two-thirds of the departments which responded and are also at universities with library schools.  Reported departmental allotments of preprofessional staff range from a high of 8.0 fulltime equivalents at Rutgers to a low of .40 fulltime equivalent at Pittsburgh.

Respondents were asked to supply the amount of hourly assistance provided by student employees in terms of fulltime equivalents. These figures are given as they were reported in Table 1 although respondents may not always have accurately converted hours worked to fulltime equivalents. Since some uncertainty surrounds the student worker data, two figures are presented for overall staff size, one including student assistant staff and the other recording total "line" staff, i.e. staff whose salaries are, presumably, line items in the budget. Both sets of overall staff figures in the Table are frequently followed by a plus sign. The plus sign reflects a positive answer to a question concerning whether the department uses staff drawn from departments other than reference to cover desk hours. This practice turned out to be much more frequent than was anticipated. Thirty-eight departments (58 percent of the respondents) supplement existing staff with contributions of time at the desk by librarians other than reference librarians, either voluntary or assigned. The numbers of staff "borrowed" from other departments varies from one for several departments to six for one department. The department "borrowing" six staff members (The University of Kentucky) was doing so on a temporary basis to cover staff shortages (as were some others). However, three departments report permanent arrangements with as many as five librarians from other departments. Unfortunately, the questionnaire failed to ask that the contribution of these supplementary staff be reported in terms of full time equivalents. Only the fact that a department has some extra help can be shown on Table 1. This was done by means of the addition of a plus-sign after the figures for total staff available. The plus sign may indicate a contribution of one to two hours per week for each "borrowed" or "drafted" librarian to as much as ten hours each week. Departments from which librarians are drawn to work at the reference desk include, for example, interlibrary loan, government documents, serials, circulation, cataloging, collection development and acquisitions. A few institutions name branch librarians and individuals from the "Director's Office" or the "library administration" as being sometime reference librarians.

The figures shown at the bottom of Table 1 for the median and average number of staff in each category (professional, preprofessionals and support staff) and for total staff are not very useful for comparative purposes. As has already been indicated, the scope of responsibility of reference departments is quite variable. The extent of the variety of functions performed will become even more clear as further data from the survey are examined.

As shown by Table 2, most of the reference departments surveyed consider themselves to be the sole or substantial providers of reference services in the humanities and the social sciences. Branches are indicated to be the primary service providers by the majority of

respondents in art and architecture, music and the sciences. At least a
few departments view themselves as having primary responsibility in each
of the areas specified.

While the range of subject coverage may not necessarily have an
impact on reference department staff size, the number of functions
assigned to the department is certainly likely to have an effect.
Summary 1 shows the variety of activities which may be carried out in
research library reference departments and the percent of respondents
which are engaged in each. As is evident from Summary 1, there are some
activities in which almost all responding reference departments are
involved, for example, online searching and some sort of general
orientation activities. Other areas for which all are responsible, but
which are not represented in the Summary nor in Table 3 which follows,
are reference collection development, reference collection maintenance,
training of students and other non-professionals, and library committee
work. Departments were asked to supply figures on the number of staff
allocated to these functions but their responses are not presented in
this report. The functions for which responses are presented in Summary
1 are those whose performance is likely to have a significant impact on
staff size. These include: responsibility for development of the
general collections of the library (done to varying degrees by 67
percent of respondents); responsibility for interlibrary borrowing and
lending (some aspect of the interlibrary loan function is performed by
up to almost half the respondents); and maintenance of central microform
collections, documents collections and newspaper collections.
Respondents were also

asked to specify whether the department had responsibility for providing reference service for the documents collection at a point separate from the reference desk.

The questionnaire asked department heads to estimate to the best of their abilities the number of professional, clerical, student assistants, and preprofessional staff (in fulltime equivalents) devoted to twenty-four specified tasks. Some found it impossible to make such estimates. These simply indicated whether or not the activity goes on in their department, but gave no indication of how much staff is devoted to it. Table 3 presents a condensed version of the responses of those department heads (N=50) who felt able to specify the number and type of FTE staff devoted to various functions.

As is explained in the footnotes to Table 3, figures for student assistant and preprofessional staff are only shown when this type of employee plays an important role in the activity under consideration. While department heads were asked about staff allocation to twenty-four specific functions, for the sake of simplicity in reporting, several tasks were grouped under broader descriptors. The staff levels given for instruction, for example, include four separately specified tasks: orientation activities (for example, tours); library instruction activities (for example, classroom or in-library presentations on sources; the manual (as opposed to computer-based) preparation of bibliographies; and the preparation of general guides and user aids. Similarly, all interlibrary lending and borrowing activities are combined although separate questions were posed concerning staff allotted to the processing of borrowing requests, the verification of

borrowing requests, the processing of lending requests, the verification

of lending requests, photoduplication of materials for other libraries

and the overall administration of the function.  Separate staffing

figures are not presented for functions common to all reference

departments (for example, development and maintenance of the collection

and staff training) or for tasks which generally do not consume a great

deal of staff time, (for example, vertical file maintenance and the

preparation of exhibits).  Separate staffing figures for labor intensive

functions which influence staff size but are not done at most libraries

do not appear in the body of the Table but are indicated in the lengthy

footnotes which follow it.  The footnotes make clear the range of tasks

which can be assigned to reference departments.  The notes specify staff

commitments to maintaining centralized newspaper collections (for

example at the University of Pennsylvania, Tulane, University of

Washington and the University of Texas); special collections or branches

(for example at the University of California at Santa Barbara, the

University of Houston and the University of Florida), copying centers

(for example, at the University of Houston) and periodical collections

(for example at Yale University).  Special collections maintained by

reference departments include maps (at Florida, the University of

Houston, the State University of New York at Stonybrook and Yale).

curriculum materials (at California/Santa Barbara) urban documents (at

Florida) and Rand Corporation and ERIC reports (at Hawaii).  Tasks less

commonly assigned to reference departments include production of the

university faculty publication list, coordination of library services

for the handicapped, and the assignment of library studies (all at

Georgetown University), indexing school and local newspapers (at Georgia Institute of Technology), supervision of the information desk (for example, at the University of Illinois), help in the operations of the Undergraduate Library (at the University of Iowa), supervision of the Publications Office (at Yale), and maintenance of the United States census tape access program (at Florida).

Aside from the provision of service to users at the desk, reference departments devote the largest amounts of professional staff time to development of the general collections (when that responsibility is borne by the department) and to instructional activities. For the thirty departments which are involved in general collection development (and which can also provide an estimate of the staff allocated to the function) the estimated staff allocation ranged from .05 FTE professional staff to 5.0 FTE. Obviously, subject area responsibilities of these departments vary considerably. Those responding that the staff allocated to general collection development ranged from 2.0 FTE librarians to 5.0 indicate either that they are selecting in all areas or that they are selecting broadly in the humanities and the social sciences. Florida, where 2.0 FTE are devoted to selection, concentrates on the social sciences. Rice, which allocates an estimated 4.0 FTE to the general selection function, also does collection development in the sciences. Most of the departments with smaller numbers of staff devoted to non-reference selection concentrate on a few, clearly defined areas.

The number of professionals performing instructional functions in responding reference departments varies from an estimated .08 FTE to an estimated 4.0 FTE.  The median for all respondents is 1.0 FTE.  (Further

description of instructional activities appears later in this report).

Almost all departments responding to the survey are involved in the

provision of online search services, but, again, estimated staffing

commitments vary considerably from department to department; i.e., from

a low of .05 FTE to a high of 3.0 FTE, with the median commitment for

all respondents falling at .63 FTE.  (Further information on online

services activities is also presented later in this report).  Staff

allocations are also shown in the body of Table 3 for interlibrary loan,

documents-related activities, microform collection maintenance and

library committee work.


The information presented in Table 3 taken together with the data in

Table 1 and other figures found in this report may assist in developing

justifications for reference staffing requests.  Comparisons among

departments are, however, not at all neat, since functions vary so

considerably.


Table 4 represents an attempt to deal with this variability.  The

professional staff sizes shown on this table were derived by subtracting

the estimated number of FTE staff committed to the various functions

reported on Table 3 which are not common to all departments; i.e.,

interlibrary lending and borrowing, maintenance of various separate

collections, provision of service at points separate from the reference

desk, general collection development, branch supervision and any other

miscellaneous tasks which happen to be assigned to reference

departments.  Estimated allocations of professional staff to instruction

and online searching were not subtracted, since almost all departments
consider themselves to be engaged in these activities (eventhough the
commitments vary widely) and since these activities are not easily
separable nowadays from general reference services.  The table lists
departments in rank order by adjusted staff size and of course it must
be borne in mind that the figures are based on subtraction of, in many
cases, very rough estimates of staffing commitments to non-standard
functions supplied by department heads.  These figures are an attempt to
provide staff sizes which may be reasonably compared among institutions.
However, the range in professional staff size is still great.  The
median for all departments is 7.4 FTE librarians who are responsible for
general reference service at a central reference desk, library
instructional activities, online search services, reference collection
development and the other tasks common to all the departments surveyed.

Table 4 also presents information on factors other than the
functions performed by reference departments which might be likely to
influence the size of the professional staff; namely, campus enrollment,
collection size, the number of reference transactions performed annually
and the number of hours of professional service provided.  To assure
comparability, only data reported to the National Center for Education
Statistics Library General Information Survey portion of Higher
Education General Information Survey (HEGIS) on reference transactions
is used.  (Only about half the respondents could supply such data.)
Separate services offered at an information desk or an undergraduate
library are also noted on Table 4 in the (as it turns out) unfounded
belief that the existence of such services might have an impact on the

amount of general reference service that must be provided and therefore on department staff size. The nature of the library system of which the reference department is a part is also indicated. Library system types were coded either 1, 2, 3, or 4. As is explained in detail in footnote 2 to the Table; the codes define in a very general way the proportion of total campus reference service provided by the central reference department of each library. In a type 1 library the central reference unit sees itself as providing essentially all services available, while a type 4 library is a highly decentralized system in which the central unit is seen to play a relatively minor role in comparison to the branches.

As might be expected, the information presented on Table 4 indicates that there is some relationship between the hours of professional service provided and the size of the reference staff. The figures also point to a very weak relationship between enrollment and staff size. However, none of the factors presented in Table 4 have significant predictive value for the number of librarians assigned to reference departments in research libraries.

## Provision of General Reference Services

Respondents were asked to specify the hours the library building is open during times of the year when normal services are maintained (i.e., not interims, holidays, summer session, etc.). They were then asked to indicate the hours during which professional reference service is usually provided. Table 5 indicates institution-by-institution the

number of hours during a typical week that the library is open as
compared with the number of hours during which general professional
reference service is available.  Open hours for responding libraries
range from 73 to 123 hours each week.  The average number of hours open
during a typical week for all libraries is approximately 99 hours.
Reference departments in responding libraries provide professional
reference service from as few as 42 hours during the week to as many as
109 hours during the week.  The average number of hours each week during
which professional reference service is available over all institutions
is 77.  The average percentage of the time that library buildings are
open that professional reference service is offered is 82 percent.  Only
four departments provide professional service during all the hours the
library is open.

Taking into account times when the reference desk is staffed by more
than one librarian, heads were also asked to specify the total number of
librarian-hours of service provided each week by their departments.  The
average number of librarian-hours of service offered each week is 112.
Taking into consideration times when the reference desk is staffed by
non-professionals, respondents were asked to indicate the total number
of person-hours of reference service provided each week by their
departments.  The average number of person-hours of service offered each
week is 153.  At only one-third of the responding departments is all
reference service provided by librarians.  Most employ non-professionals
at the reference desk during some hours.  On the average, 81 percent of
the reference service provided is professional.  Figures 1 through 3
show the pattern of reference staffing in research libraries in relation

to building hours on Mondays through Thursdays, on Saturdays and on Sundays. Hours during which professional service is provided are charted, along with hours when two librarians (or in a few cases, three librarians) are scheduled for service.

Table 5 also reflects the weekly desk-hour workload of the typical reference librarian in an academic research library. The questionnaire asked department heads to specify the average number of hours worked at the reference desk by full-time librarians with normal responsibilities during a typical week. Reported desk-hour workloads range from a high of 33.5 hours each week to a low of 7.7 hours. The average number of hours worked at the desk each week by the typical librarian over all institutions is 13.6.

## Productivity

While it might certainly be interesting to arrive at some norm for the number of questions a reference librarian can answer during a given time (for example, in a week), data collected by this survey did not make possible any such calculations. In theory we have a national reporting mechanism which would provide us with the ability to collect standardized data on reference transactions in academic libraries. The Higher Education General Information Survey/Library General Information Survey (HEGIS/LIBGIS) of the National Center for Education Statistics contains a question on reference transactions per typical week. Respondents to the survey reported here were asked to supply HEGIS/LIBGIS data for their departments for two points in time.

The intent of this question was to ascertain the change in the amount of reference service provided by the various departments since the last survey and to gather information which could be used to generate some estimate of reference librarian productivity. Only 19 reference departments could provide HEGIS/LIBGIS data for two points in time. All but five departments show an increase in questions answered which ranges from 11 to 118 percent. Thirty-two reference departments (almost half the respondents) could report HEGIS data on reference transactions for 1982. However, the variations among institutions (from a low of 456 transactions reported by one institution for a typical week to a high of 13,037 reported by another) suggests that the data are not really comparable, despite the supposed use of standard definitions and collection methods. Any estimates of reference-librarian productivity based on these data would not seem likely to have much validity. Table 6 presents HEGIS data on reference transactions and also annual tabulations made according to local policies and procedures from institutions which could not report statistics submitted to the national survey. Reference service is not uniformly increasing at all institutions. In fact, about one third of those reporting statistics of any kind for reference questions answered in 1977/78 as compared with those answered in 1981/82 indicate a decrease in the number of transactions taking place in their departments.

Related General Services

Approximately 45 percent (N=29) of the departments who responded to the survey have information desks separate from the reference desk located in their libraries. About three-quarters of the existing

information desks (N=21) are administered and, frequently partially

staffed, by members of the reference department. Six information desks

are supervised by the reference department head and in many other cases

supervision is the responsibility of a designated member of the

reference staff, usually a librarian, but occasionally a

non-professional. About a third of the desks are staffed exclusively

with reference personnel. Approximately half draw staff from

departments other than reference who either volunteer or have a part of

their time assigned to the function. The rest do not specify the

source from which staff are drawn. At twenty-three desks service is

provided largely or exclusively by non-professional staff, but

librarians give information service at a point separate from the

reference desk in thirteen libraries. Hours of service at information

desks range from 20 per week to 180 per week. Most are located in the

area of the main card catalog and all but three are prepared to offer

catalog assistance. Only eight also provide ready reference services.


SPECIAL REFERENCE SERVICES


Bibliographic Instruction


The first set of questions concerning bibliographic instruction

included in the survey instrument were aimed at discovering the degree

of responsibility for the library's general instructional efforts which

is borne by reference departments. Eight of the responding libraries

(12 percent) reported the existence of a separate bibliographic

instruction section at their institutions. Four of these libraries
indicate that this separate section has primary responsibility for the
library's general instruction program, but in all but two libraries (the
University of Alabama and Georgia Institute of Technology), the
reference department is nevertheless involved in a wide variety of
bibliographic instruction activities. For those libraries which
identify separate B/I sections, the staffing levels in fulltime
equivalents were given as follows.

| Institution | Staffing Levels of Bibliographic Instruction Sections | | | | |
|---|---|---|---|---|---|
| | Professional | Clerical | Pre-Prof. | Students | Total |
| Alabama | 1.00 | | 2.6 | | 3.60 |
| Arizona | 2.00 | | | | 2.00 |
| Arizona State | 1.00 | | | | 1.00 |
| Connecticut | 1.00 | 6.5 | | 1.00 | 8.50 |
| Georgia Tech. | 1.50 | | .75 | 2.25 | 4.50 |
| Indiana | 1.00 | | | | 1.00 |
| Penn. State | 1.00 | | | | 1.00 |
| Washington St. | .25 | | | .25 | .50 |

Three of the "sections" are one-person operations.  At Alabama and
Pennsylvania State, the library instruction librarian reports to the
library director; at Indiana the coordinator reports to the public
services director.  Although Berkeley does not appear in the list above
because of its own choice of responses, it could be thought of as having
a separate one-person "section", since there is staff position reporting
to the public services director responsible for instructional
activities.  The heads of instructional sections which have additional
staff assigned report either to the library director (one case), to the
public services director (two cases), or to a public service division
head (one case).  Instruction librarians who are not part of the
reference department are either involved with reference in essentially
all instructional activities performed or are assigned very particular
functions.  At Pennsylvania State the independent instructional
coordinator does all tours for off-campus groups; at Berkeley this
individual works with faculty and graduate students and develops user
aids.  At the University of Arizona reference and the instructional
section cooperate to provide tours and freshman and lower division
orientations and instruction.  At Connecticut the instruction section
has exclusive responsibility for tours and user aids and is also
somewhat involved with the faculty.  The Washington State bibliographic
instruction section handles all tours, freshman orientation and
instruction and new librarian orientations.

When asked to describe the level of their department's responsibility generally for bibliographic instruction, about 17 percent of responding department heads indicated that their department had sole responsibility for the function and 66 percent indicate "substantial" responsibility. When asked of there is "a [person in their library] who is assigned primary responsibility for management and coordination of library instruction and orientation", 74 percent of the survey respondents answered in the affirmative (This percentage includes the libraries which indicate the existence of separate bibliographic instruction "section".) In 28 cases the library instruction coordinator is a reference librarian reporting to the head of reference and in 9 cases the coordinator is the head of reference. There are a few unusual situations: for example at Rutgers, the coordinator is a reference librarian reporting to the public services director. At Texas the head of reference looks after instruction for the main library. At Temple, three librarians have major instructional responsibilities: the head of reference is in charge of overall coordination, one reference librarian coordinates the workbook program and course-related instruction and another coordinates the credit course offered and develops user guides.

The heavy involvement of reference departments in instructional work is borne out by the list of activities on Table 7 for which reference departments consider themselves to be primarily responsible. Undergraduate libraries exist at about 29 percent of the responding libraries and, as is shown in Table 7, they frequently take primary responsibility for freshman orientation and instruction and, to a lesser extent, for lower division course-related library skills instruction.

At several libraries, independent bibliographic instruction sections or librarians also play a leading role in introducing new students to the library. Those reference departments which are responsible for freshman orientation and instruction employ a variety of approaches. A list of techniques showing the percentage of respondents who employ them is presented in Summary 2.

As indicated by Table 7, aside from freshman instruction, the only area of user education in which reference departments may not always take the lead is in the development of user aids describing automated library systems. At those institutions where online circulation or catalog systems have been implemented, other library bodies, such as systemwide committees have been involved in preparing system guides and instructions.

The breadth of instructional activities pursued by reference departments is shown in Summary 3. Based on comparison with data collected in the 1977 survey, there appears to have been a strong increase in reference department involvement in semester-length course offerings in basic library skills and in specialized bibliography and also an increase in the presentation of library workshops for freshmen. Various other teaching activities not specified by the questionnaire were cited by department heads. Faculty workshops are offered, for example, at the University of California-Irvine. At UCLA, the reference department provides specific courses of instruction at the request of faculty in the humanities and the social sciences and it initiates general seminars on topics such as international relations and history.

Reference librarians at the University of Chicago edit an orientation newspaper for students. Cornell offers graduate seminars in library research and a two-hour non-course-related workshop on the library for new graduate students and faculty. The reference department at the University of Florida engages in a variety of instructional enterprises, including for example, faculty and new graduate student seminars, instruction for foreign students and a two-week summer mini-course for entering minority students. The reference departments at the Universities of Kentucky and Delaware offer computer-aided instruction in library skills. Stanford and Harvard reference librarians provide individualized counseling sessions fore graduate students. Several departments offer regular specialized demonstrations of in-house and commercial information retrieval services.

As with reference transactions, survey respondents were asked to supply standardized data on the level of instructional activity for their department during selected years. The earliest year for which such data are available is 1978/79, since the question on group transactions was not added to the HEGIS/LIBGIS Survey until fall 1979. The questionnaire asked for HEGIS data on total group transactions for the earliest year reported and for 1981/82. Since it was expected that not all respondents would be able to supply HEGIS data, a second question was included asking for a subjective estimate of the percent change in reference department instructional activity over the preceding five-year period. Fifty-nine departments answered one question or the other. Their answers appear on Table 8. The range of HEGIS data respondents supply on group transactions, like those supplied on reference transactions, is great enough to make their use for comparisons of productivity among institutions seem suspect. It appears likely that some departments reported the number of group meetings and others reported the number of individuals contacted through group meetings. Obviously the question should have been more clearly specified. If it can be assumed that departments are consistent in what they report for the two years requested, perhaps comparisons of the percent of change among departments have some validity. Such percentages can be computed for only twenty departments. All but three show an increase in instructional activity. Subjective estimates of change were provided by 26 departments. Twenty-four reported an increase. When asked what new services had been initiated by their departments during the last five years, 22 departments reported significantly expanded activities in user education and several others reported instructional programs under development. The reference department at University of California at Irvine, for example, has begun offering instruction to doctoral students in the School of Social Sciences. Reference librarians at SUNY-Buffalo have been involved in some three-credit course offerings: research skills in English literature at the graduate level and similar courses in history at both the graduate and the undergraduate level. A slide tape, "Library Research in German, Spanish and French Literature," has also been developed. The department at the University of Virginia has begun to make formal library instruction available to graduate students in the humanities and the social sciences. At Notre Dame, reference librarians provide a tour/worksheet program which is required of all freshmen. Credit courses are now being taught by reference librarians at

Pennsylvania State, Louisiana State, Indiana and the University of Missouri and one was in the planning stages at both Johns Hopkins and the University of New Mexico at the time of the survey. Johns Hopkins also had plans for a program of weekly workshops for undergraduates, especially freshmen. Louisiana State was working on programs for new graduate students targeted at specific academic departments and for orientation activities for new faculty. Bibliographic instruction for students in the Honors College was being developed at Oregon and librarians were also exploring possibilities for a library instruction module in English composition and research courses. Reference departments at both Pennsylvania State and Florida expect to take an active role in online catalog user training.

Despite the various indications of the expansion of the teaching role of reference departments presented in this report, very few respondents indicate that instructional programs have formal budgetary support at their institutions. Only 10 libraries (15 percent of the sample) gave a positive answer when asked if instruction program expenditures are a line item in the library budget. Most of these libraries did not supply information on salaries and wages, but did supply some on the budget for equipment and supplies. The combined supplies and equipment budgets for the eight libraries who responded to this question ranged from $500 to $14,000, with the average budgeted amount being approximately $4,000. The high figure is at the University of California-Berkeley and it is specifically indicated to cover the expense of producing instructional publications.

Online Search Services

Although many reference departments were just getting started in online information retrieval when the 1977 survey was taken and several have only initiated services some time within the last eight years, almost all the departments queried in 1983 see themselves as having significant responsibilities in this area.  When asked to specify the locus of responsibility for online search services in their libraries, 15 percent of the respondents indicated that the reference department has sole responsibility for this function and another 76 percent indicated that reference has "a substantial responsibility" although searches are also conducted in the branches.  At Yale, however, where the department had only recently begun search activities, almost all searching was done by the branches at the time of the survey.  Searching at Syracuse was formerly done be reference, but has been transferred to a full-time search analyst (the Head of Media Services) who reports to the Associate Director for Collections.  A fulltime online searching coordinator (who reports to the public services director) also handles searching at Brigham Young.  Washington State has a somewhat unique arrangement in that its quite substantial amount of searching is done entirely by reference librarians who are responsible to a coordinator outside the department for this part of their work.

To get a clearer idea of what department heads might construe as "a substantial responsibility" for online searching, they were also asked to provide statistics on the number of searches done during the previous year (1981/82) both by the reference department and by all libraries in

the system combined.  Six departments (shown in Table 9) report that
reference has sole responsibility for searching and also do not supply
statistics on reference department versus systemwide searches which are
inconsistent with that response (a few claim sole responsibility and
then supply statistics on searches done in other units of the library
which are sometimes greater than the number reported for the reference
department alone.)  The average percentage of searching done by
reference departments over all libraries is close to 50 percent of the
total searching done in the system as a whole.

We were interested not only in how the online search function is
organized within research libraries and in the role reference
departments typically play in that organization, but also in how the
activity is organized within reference departments.  Most departments
(77 percent) specify that "several librarians spend a part of their
time" doing searching; only three departments say that designated
librarians spend all or most of their time searching.  In terms of how
searches are assigned, 22 percent of departments indicate that
librarians are prepared to search all databases, but two-thirds indicate
that librarians "usually perform searches in a subject area with which
they are familiar or on databases with which they have had experience."
Three libraries employ non-librarians to do searching.  Searches are
almost always scheduled by appointment and those libraries who do offer
on-demand searching qualify their indication of the availability of this
service with phrases like "occasionally" or "if time is available."
Johns Hopkins reports that searches are promised within a week and the
client is not usually present for the search.  At the time of the survey

no departments allowed users to do their own searching, although there was considerable interest in the possibilities.

Besides the percentage of total library system searching done by reference departments, Table 9 also records the number of searches done by individual departments in each of the five years from 1977/78 to 1981/82. The definition of a search used in the survey was developed by the Machine-Aided Reference Services Section of RASD and is widely accepted: "the interactive access by computer to as many databases as the searcher considers necessary to conclude the search." The median number of searches done by reference departments in 1981/82 is 378. When year-to year changes for individual departments are examined, 49 percent show a steady increase in searches done each year. An additional 12 percent show a general upward trend, despite the occasional yearly fluctuation downward which might be due to the loss of a trained searcher or some other ephemeral circumstance. Searching has steadily decreased in only 3 percent of departments and has shown a general downward trend in only an additional 5 percent. For four reference departments (7 percent of respondents) online activity peaked in 1979/80 (midway through the five-year period) and then decreased. Seven departments (12 percent of respondents) have an irregular pattern of searching volume in which no trend is evident and the remaining 14 percent (eight reference departments) provided only one year of data on searching volume.

Table 10 shows the estimated number of staff devoted to online searching by each department, the number of searches done in 1981/82, and the broad range in numbers of searches per FTE librarian per year which can be computed from these numbers. The median over all departments of searches per FTE per librarian per year is 657.

Most departments surveyed (75 percent) are recovering either full costs for searching for their own faculty and students or are recovering full costs plus an added service charge (See Summary 4). A few (10.8 percent), charge a flat fee which may be a subsidy depending on the cost of the search and some departments (12.3 percent) subsidize searching. At most institutions students and faculty are treated in the same way. However, two institutions try to give students a break: the University of California at Irvine gives students $10 of searching free when funds are available and the University of Delaware charges them only half the 15 percent surcharge which faculty must pay. At two institutions faculty with grant support pay full cost, while other university clients receive some sort of subsidy.

Off-campus users are treated in a variety of ways. Eleven institutions indicate they do not serve non-university users and nine institutions treat all non-university users in the same manner as the campus clientele. One institution indicates non-university clients are referred to a separate fee-based service operation. Three institutions deny them the subsidy afforded other users and one adds on yet another

$10, Four institutions charge off-campus patrons for the time of the searcher. Hourly rates reported were $12.50, $25.00 and $30.00. Sixteen departments assess an additional fixed charge which can be a flat fee ranging from $5.00 to $25.00 or a percentage ranging from 25 percent to 50 percent. One charges outside users its regular 15 percent surcharge plus an additional 50 percent plus a $10 flat fee. One department $20 per hour (with a half-hour minimum) plus 15 percent of the cost of the search. Another charges an additional $15 plus 17 percent of the search cost.

Fourteen of the departments reporting enforce different fee structures for different categories of outside users (See Summary 5 for a display of the practices in use at the time of the survey). About half these departments assess heavier additional charges for for-profit organizations.

The cost of using commercially-produced online information retrieval systems for ready reference purposes may become more of an issue for reference departments as the number of databases increases and librarians grow more accustomed to resorting to the terminal to save their own time and that of their users in answering routine questions.

At the time of the survey 70 percent of the participating departments answered "yes" to the question of whether they used online systems to answer ready reference questions and to verify citations for patrons. An additional 6 percent reported that they had plans to do so. Forty reference departments (or 62 percent of the respondents)

report that online ready reference searching done for patrons is free of
charge. Two indicate they do online searches to answer routine patron
queries only occasionally and one library does charge non-affiliated
users for any searches done in connection with their inquiries. Five
libraries charge patrons for all ready-reference searches done. Forty
reference departments (35 percent of respondents) go beyond the use of
online databases strictly for ready reference and verification purposes
and will also do short subject searches for patrons in response to
routine queries. Three departments indicate they do so only
occasionally and one does so only when IAC Search Helper can be used.

Only fewer than half those departments who do online ready reference
searching provided any statistics on the number of such searches done
per year. As can be seen from Table 11, most of those who report
statistics indicate an increase in their activity from whenever they
began keeping records to 1980/81, although for most the number of
searches reported is not very great. Some explanation for the low level
of online ready reference activity reflected in the survey report may
be found in the lack of convenient arrangements for searching to be done
as part of the reference interview. Only 23 percent of the departments
who do ready reference searching are equipped to do so at the reference
desk. Searching is done in the reference department office or in
separate search service offices located in fairly close proximity to the
reference room in 60 percent of the departments. For 22 percent of
departments who try to do ready reference searching, search terminals
are located in distant and inconvenient locations. (These percentages
do not add to 100 since some departments have more than one search

location).

The survey sought to determine the cost of supporting online ready reference searching not charged to patrons both in the reference department alone and systemwide. The annual cost for searching done in reference departments ranged from "minimal" to an estimates $11,000 to $12,000 in the twenty-nine departments who answered this question. The median of costs reported was $1,000. A far smaller number of respondents felt able to estimate the cost to their libraries for ready reference searching done in all units. Costs reported ranged from $500 to $25,000, with the median for the ten departments answering being $2,550. Costs to libraries of reference department online ready reference searches are frequently absorbed by general library accounts. Examples of accounts charged included: "supplies and services," the "general expenditure budget," and the "Director's Office budget." Three libraries charge these expenses to book funds and several do have a separate fund specifically allocated for this purpose.

Online services, like instructional activities, have been a growth area for reference departments over the last several years. At the time of the survey many libraries were considering various new initiatives in automated information retrieval. A few were beginning to plan for end-user searching and some were contemplating the application of microcomputers to specific reference problems. Two plans for microcomputer use were to answer directional questions and to provide local information to users. It seems likely that the high interest in the use of microcomputers has resulted in additional reference-related applications in research libraries which have been put in place since the survey was done or are now under development.

REFERENCE DEPARTMENT PERSONNEL AND GENERAL ADMINISTRATION

Reference heads were asked to provide various information concerning the characteristics of librarians working in their departments, including their sex, years of experience, and the degrees they hold. According to Association of Research Library statistics for fiscal 1983[4], 63.7 percent of research librarians are women. Based on the data collected in this survey, reference librarianship is a marginally more feminine branch of academic research librarianship: 68.5 percent of the librarians for whom sex was reported are female. Since ARL statistics[5] for fiscal 1984 reported librarians' experience levels using the same ranges as were employed in this survey, 1984 ARL data instead of 1983 data are used to compare the experience distribution of reference librarians surveyed to the experience distribution of research librarians generally. Reference departments have a slightly higher percentage of librarians with three or fewer years of experience than are found in all branches of research librarianship (15.6 percent as compared with 11.6 percent). There is also a slightly higher percentage of reference librarians with 4 to 7 years of experience (21.1 percent as compared with 16.9 percent for research librarians in general). Although it might be supposed that reference departments serve as training grounds for other positions in research libraries or that "burnout" might keep turnover in departments steady, the majority of reference librarians have passed the time when tenure is usually granted in academic institutions and have more than seven years of experience.

As to the educational attainment of reference librarians in research libraries, the statistics are as follows:  29 percent have a subject master's degree in addition to their professional degree; a little less than 7 percent have a doctorate in addition to the MLS; 7.5 percent are at work on a second master's and 2.5 percent are enrolled in a doctoral program; about 2 percent hold a bachelor's degree in library science; less than 1 percent hold a higher degree but no professional degree and a few have the library science bachelor's and a subject master's.  The prevalence of advanced training in academic disciplines may be a little lower than might be expected, considering that 67 percent of the departments in the survey have responsibility for development of library collections in various subject areas.

The extension of reference functions into new areas such as online services and bibliographic instruction has led to a certain degree of specialization in the jobs of general reference librarians and to delegation of responsibilities within departments.  Although in forty percent of departments "administrative responsibility for the department is entirely in the hands of the head," in the others, the head shares responsibility with one or more designees.  The percentage of departments with the most commonly designated specialized positions is shown below:

Department with an Assistant Head                                    21%

  Administrative Authority is shared with this Individual only       9%

Departments with an Online Services Coordinator                     42%

Departments with an Instructional Services Coordinator              29%

Departments with a Reference Collection Development Coordinator     17%


The duties usually assigned to individuals holding the positions listed above (and other less frequently occurring positions of responsibility) are described in the introduction to the policy and and administrative documents collected as part of this survey which are published separately.  Sample position descriptions are also included among the documents reproduced in that publication[6] along with general policy and procedure manuals, library and reference department organization charts, reference collection development policies, general online services policies, and online ready reference service policies.

Other information relating to the general administration of reference departments requested by the questionnaire included the size of the book budget and the number of volumes in the reference collection. The information which respondents were able to supply is reported on Table 12.  About a quarter of the respondents can supply no information whatever about their budget for either monographs or serials.  As with any of the information which respondents failed to supply in this survey, the absence of the data may simply mean that the individual answering the questionnaire did not know the information offhand and could not take the time to look it up.  Some of the departments indicate

in response to this particular question, however, that budgetary
information is not supplied because the reference department does not
actually have a formal budget allocation.  Fifteen departments (about 21
percent) can provide a budget figure for monographs, but indicate that
reference is not allocated a separate serials budget.  Looking at all
the figures provided for monographs budgets, including those for
departments which also provided a budget figure for serials, the median
monographs budget for all departments reporting is $20,000.  Thirty-one
departments provide a total allocation figure.  In five cases separate
breakdowns for serials and monographs are not shown and, for Texas A & M
and the University of Texas, the serials allocation is specified to
apply to new materials only.  (Although the University of Washington
did not say so, the size of the serials allocation given suggests that
it too applies only to new purchases.)  The median total reference book
budget allocation (presumably for both new purchases and continuing
commitments) was about $64,000 in fiscal year 1983.

Collections range greatly in size from a low of 5,000 volumes to a
high of almost 78,000 volumes.  The median reference collection size is
about 22,700 volumes.  Variations in both budget allocations and
collection size may certainly have to do with how the reference
department's role in the library system is defined in relation to other
collections.  Obviously, space may also be a strong determinant for
collection size.

As part of the general review of administrative practices in
reference departments, the survey asked for information on the means

used to evaluate both staff and services. In 60 percent of departments, staff evaluation is done by the department head acting alone or, in two cases with the advice of the assistant head. Peer review is brought into play in a few of these departments when a promotion is at issue and, in one department, peer and user opinions are sought at the time of the third and sixth year reviews. In 21 percent of the departments peer review is a routine part of the evaluation process. At three institutions the views of peers and users are regularly sought by the department head as part of the evaluation process. One department claims evaluation is based only on input from peers and users and two others rely on peer evaluation only. In two departments the individual occupying the position above the reference head in the administrative hierarchy is responsible for formal evaluation of the reference staff. Two departments report that no formal evaluation of job performance takes place at their institution. Several units employ job performance measures in addition to the ones already mentioned: a few seek comments from other librarians in the system to judge the work of reference librarians; a few others have librarians write self-evaluations.

Only twelve reference departments describe any formal mechanisms in place or expected for the evaluation of reference service programs (two of these employ two different methodologies). Four departments indicated that the evaluation of reference services was part of a larger institutional self-study or planning program: two, for example, cited their library's participation in ARL Office of Management's Public Service Self-Study Program. Two employ departmental "self-study," one reports progress according to yearly "measurable" goals and objectives, one employs "statistics, " i.e., presumably purely quantitative measures and one relies on user surveys. Four others respond that they evaluate only selected aspects of the reference program, for example, online services or elements of the instructional program. Despite continual calls in the library literature for measures of the quality and not just the quantity of reference service provided, the application of such measures is not at all a routine occurrence, at least in the academic research library setting.

A FEW CHANGES OBSERVED SINCE THE 1977 SURVEY

As has already been mentioned above there has been recognizable growth at most institutions in online searching and in instructional activities. Perhaps because of the increase in activity in these areas, most reference departments have grown in size over the five years previous to when the survey was taken. Only 6 out of the 47 libraries who responded to this question had lost professionals during the five-year period 1977/78-1982/83. For departments which gained professional staff, the average number of FTE librarians added was 1.9 FTE. Forty percent of respondents had also added an average of 1.8 FTE clerical staff. (Table 13 details staff changes institution-by-by-institution).

There has also been a decline in the average desk-hour workload for the typical reference librarian. The 1977 survey found that reference librarians normally worked 17.8 hours each week at the desk, whereas this survey found that number to have decreased to 13.6 hours per week.

CONCLUSION

Despite careful attempts to be more specific in questioning and to quantify factors which might influence staff size, this survey was no more successful than the 1977 survey in arriving at norms for reference staff size or at isolating external factors which might influence staff size.  The survey also failed to arrive at norms for reference librarian productivity or for departmental levels of instructional activity.  Hard comparative data on a variety of factors appears to be either unavailable or uncollectable.  The length of the questionnaire was dictated by the information needs which the discussion group members who participated in its design perceived to be important to themselves and to their colleagues at other institutions.  Many of the respondents may not have had much of the data ready to hand and they may not have wished to compile or to search for it.  It seems likely, though, that at some institutions, certain quantitative facts about reference departments are simply not known to department heads.  Where national reporting mechanisms exist, (e.g., through HEGIS for reference and group transactions) they appear to be inconsistently applied.  Some potentially useful, or at least suggestive, facts and figures about reference services in university libraries have emerged from this survey.  On the whole, however, the 1983 survey, like the 1977 survey, underlines the diversities in organization and function of university library reference departments rather the similarities.

Footnotes

[1]Paula D. Watson ed.  <u>Reference Policy and Administrative Documents</u> (Chicago:  American Library Association; Reference and Adult Services Division, 1985) 51 1., 851 pp. (in 9 microfiche)

[2]Results of the previous survey were published in Paula D. Watson and Martha Landis, <u>Working Paper on Staffing, Services and Organization</u> <u>of Reference Departments in Large Academic Libraries</u> (Arlington, VA: ERIC Document Reproduction Service, 1978) ED 142 184 and Paula D. Watson and Martha Landis, <u>Report on Reference Services in Large Academic</u> <u>Libraries</u> (Arlington, VA:  ERIC Document Reproduction Service, 1978), ED 149775.

[3]The survey questionnaire was developed with the help of the following members of the ALA Reference and Adult Services Division Reference Services in Large Research Libraries Discussion Group:  Jane Bryan (University of Pennsylvania), Carol Christensen (University of Minnesota), Carolyn Dusenbury (Arizona State University), Peter Malanchuk (University  of Florida), Julie Miller (University of Pennsylvania), Virginia Parr (University of Cincinnati).  Marjorie Karlson (University of Massachusetts; Reference Services in Medium-Sized Libraries Discussion Group) reviewed the questionnaire.  Thanks are due also to Mary Jo Lynch of the ALA Office of Research who provided useful advice.  Andrew M. Hansen, Executive Director of RASD, and the members of the RASD Publications Committee have patiently encouraged this project.

[4]Association of Research Libraries.  _ARL Annual Salary Survey 1982_
(Washington; Association of Research Libraries, 1982), p. 28

[5]_____.  ARL Annual Salary Survey 1983,
Washington:  Association of Research Libraries, 1983), p. 28

[6]Watson.  _Reference Policy and Administrative Documents_, pp. xiv-xx
of the introduction and pp. 37-164 of the documents.

Tables

Table 1. Research Library Reference Department Staff Size

| Institution | FTE Librs. | FTE Clerical | FTE Pre Prof. | FTE Stud. Asst. | Suppl. Staff (head ct.)[1] | Total Line Staff[2] (FTE) | Total Staff (FTE) |
|---|---|---|---|---|---|---|---|
| Alabama | 7.0 | 3.0 | | | | 10.00 | 10.00 |
| Arizona | 10.0[3] | 9.0 | 4.00 | 6.0 | (2) | 23.0+ | 29.0+ |
| Arizona State | 14.0 | 3.0 | | 3.0 | (4) | 17.0+ | 20.0+ |
| BYU | 3.0 | 3.0 | 4.50 | 2.5 | | 10.5 | 13.0 |
| Br. Colum. | Divisional system | | | | | | |
| Brown[4] | 11.0 | 2.0 | | | (3) | 13.0+ | 13.0+ |
| UC-Berkeley | 11.5 | 2.0 | .75 | 1.0 | (1) | 14.25+ | 15.25+ |
| UC-Davis | Divisional system | | | | | | |
| UC-Irvine | 7.0 | 3.0 | | | (3) | 10.0+ | 10.0+ |
| UCLA | 10.0 | 8.0 | 1.00 | 3.7 | | 19.0 | 22.7 |
| UC-S.Diego | 9.95 | 2.0 | | .5 | (2) | 11.95+ | 12.45+ |
| UC-S.Barbara | 10.00 | 8.5 | | 8.0 | (1) | 18.5+ | 26.5+ |
| Case Western[5] | 3.5 | 0.0 | 2.00 | 1.0 | (2) | 5.5+ | 6.5+ |
| Chicago | 6.0 | 2.0 | | 1.7 | (1) | 8.0+ | 9.7+ |
| Cincinnati | 10.75 | 6.0 | | 3.0 | | 16.75 | 19.75 |
| Colorado | 9.0 | 3.0 | | | | 12.0 | 12.0 |
| Columbia | 6.0 | 0.0 | 1.00 | 1.0 | | 7.0 | 8.0 |
| Connecticut | 8.0 | 1.0 | | | (5) | 9.0+ | 9.0 |
| Cornell | 7.0 | 3.5 | | .50 | (5) | 10.5+ | 11.0+ |
| Delaware[6] | 15.75 | 11.5 | | 4.00 | (1) | 27.25+ | 31.25+ |
| Duke | 6.75 | 1.0 | 1.00 | 1.00 | | 8.75 | 9.75 |
| Florida | 14.50 | 8.0 | | 5.75 | | 22.50 | 28.25 |
| Georgetown | 6.5 | 2.5 | .50 | 2.50 | (1) | 9.50 | 12.00 |
| Ga. Tech. | 7.0 | 1.0 | | .50 | (4) | 8.0 | 8.50 |
| Guelph | Divisional | | | | | | |
| Harvard | 4.0 | 1.0 | | | | 5.0 | 5.0 |
| Hawaii[7] | 8.0 | 2.0 | 2.00 | 3.00 | | 12.0 | 15.0 |
| Houston[8] | 14.0 | 22.5 | | 11.25 | | 36.5 | 47.75 |
| Illinois | 7.0 | 2.0 | 2.25 | 2.25 | (2) | 11.25+ | 13.50+ |
| Indiana | 6.0 | 4.0 | 3.00 | 1.75 | | 13.00 | 14.75 |
| Iowa | 10.5 | 2.5 | | 6.00 | | 13.00 | 19.00 |
| J. Hopkins[9] | 6.0 | 3.0 | | 2.00 | (2) | 9.00+ | 11.00+ |
| Kansas | 8.5 | 1.0 | | .50 | (1) | 9.50+ | 10.00+ |
| Kentucky | 6.0 | 1.0 | 2.00 | | (6) | 9.00 | 9.00 |
| LSU | 9.0 | 4.0 | 2.50 | 4.00 | | 15.50 | 19.50 |
| Manitoba[10] | 11.35 | 10.0 | | 1.80 | | 21.35 | 23.15 |
| Massachusetts | 10.5 | 3.0 | | 3.20 | (1) | 13.50 | 16.70 |
| Mich. St. | 12.0 | 3.0 | | 3.20 | (1) | 15.00+ | 18.20+ |
| Minnesota[11] | 5.8 | 5.25 | | .90 | (5) | 11.05+ | 11.95+ |
| Missouri[12] | Essentially a divisional system | | | | | | |
| N. Mexico | 13.0 | 1.5 | | 3.60 | (3) | 14.50 | 18.10+ |
| NYU[13] | 8.0 | 3.0 | | | | 11.00 | 11.00 |
| No. Carolina | Divisional system | | | | | | |
| N. Car. St. | 6.0 | 4.0 | | 4.00 | | 10.0 | 14.0 |
| Northwestern | 7.5 | 1.5 | | 3.00 | (2) | 9.0+ | 12.00+ |
| Notre Dame | 6.5 | 7.0 | | .75 | (1) | 13.5+ | 14.25+ |

| Institution | FTE Librs. | FTE Clerical | FTE Pre Prof. | FTE Stud. Asst. | Suppl. Staff (head ct.)[1] | Total Line Staff[2] (FTE) | Total Staff (FTE) |
|---|---|---|---|---|---|---|---|
| Oklahoma | 9.0 | 5.0 | 4.00 | 4.00 | (2) | 14.0+ | 18.0+ |
| Oregon | 11.25[14] | 1.5 | | 1.75 | (2) | 12.75+ | 14.50+ |
| Penn. | 10.5 | 3.0 | | 6.00 | | 13.50 | 19.50 |
| Penn. St. | 10.5 | 4.0 | | 3.00 | | 14.50 | 17.50 |
| Pittsburgh | 8.0 | 2.0 | .40 | | (1) | 10.40+ | 10.40 |
| Purdue | No Central Reference Department | | | | | | |
| Queen's | 4.66 | 4.00 | | | (2) | 8.66+ | 8.66+ |
| Rice | 6.0 | | | .25 | (1) | 6.25+ | 6.25+ |
| Rutgers[15] | 8.0 | 2.0 | 8.00 | | (4) | 18.00+ | |
| So. Cal. | 7.0 | 3.0 | | | | 10.00 | 10.00 |
| SIU | Divisional System | | | | | | |
| Stanford | 6.00 | 8.00 | 4.00 | | (4) | 18.00 | 18.00 |
| SUNY-Buff.[16] | 6.30 | 1.0 | 1.00 | 4.00 | (3) | 8.30 | 12.30 |
| SUNY-Stbr. | 13.25 | 8.0 | | 5.00 | (1) | 21.25+ | 26.25+ |
| Syracuse | 10.00 | 3.0 | | 17.00 | | 13.00 | 30.00 |
| Temple[17] | 11.45 | 5.0 | | 1.33 | (2) | 11.95+ | 13.28+ |
| Tennessee | 12.00 | 3.0 | 1.80 | 3.20 | (2) | 16.80+ | 20.00+ |
| Texas | 10.00 | 17.0 | | 3.00 | (5) | 27.00+ | 30.00 |
| Texas A&M | 14.00 | 10.0 | | 4.00 | (2) | 24.00+ | 28.00+ |
| Tulane | | 9.0 | | | | | |
| Vanderbilt[18] | 11.00 | 1.0 | | | (1) | 12.00 | 12.00 |
| Virginia | 6.00 | 2.50 | | 1.50 | | 8.50 | 10.00 |
| Va. Poly. | Divisional system | | | | | | |
| U. of Wash. | 4.95 | 4.00 | 1.44 | .48 | | 10.39 | 10.87 |
| Wash. St. | 10.00 | 3.00 | | 6.75 | | 13.00 | 19.75 |
| Wisconsin | 5.0 | 3.50 | .75 | .50 | | 9.25 | 9.75 |
| Yale | 5.50 | 8.50 | | 15.00 | | 14.00 | 29.00 |
| Average for all libraries | 8.66 | 4.30 | 2.28 | | | | 16.12 |
| Median for all libraries | 8 | 3 | 2 | | | | 13 |

General Explanation of Terms: Clerical is a generic term which refers to all non-professional staff except for student assistants or pre-professionals (i.e., library school students.) Paraprofessionals are included in this class.

[1]This column gives the headcount of librarians from other departments who rotate desk duty in reference departments. Since the respondents were not asked to specify their contribution in terms of FTE, their contribution in the figure for total line staff can be shown only by a plus (+) sign.

[2]Total line staff represents the addition of columns 1, 2, & 3. The next column gives a total staff figure which includes student assistants. This figure may not be entirely reliable since respondents may not always have supplied figures for students in terms of full time equivalents.

[3]Figure does not include the head.

[4]The questions are answered as though there is only one building since the reference department consists of all librarians and services in both the general and the Sciences Library.

[5]The library system consists of two major libraries: one for sciences and one for social sciences and humanities. The answers given apply only to the Freiburger Library (the social science and humanities library).

[6]The Reference Department at Delaware did not supply data in terms of full time equivalent staff allocated to the various functions it performs which include documents processing and reference, interlibrary lending and borrowing, and the supervision of four branches, namely Agriculture, Chemistry, Marine Studies and Physics.

[7]Report is for the General Reference Department in the Hamilton Library (the research facility) which emphasizes humanities and social sciences.

[8]The totals for the University of Houston include staff (professional, non-professional and student) who are providing service in branch libraries which are under the administration of the reference department.

[9]The central reference desk handles social sciences and humanities and there is a separate science reference point. The respondent indicated that the answers apply to both service points since "we are all one reference department."

[10]Reference Services and Collections Department consists of 4 divisions: Reference Section (with Reference librarians who are bibliographers); Interlibrary Loan and Microforms section, Bibliography Section (one bibliographer provides six hours per week of reference desk service) and the Government Publication Section.

[11]Answers are for the Wilson Library (one of five major libraries) in the system. Wilson Library houses most of the social sciences and humanities collections and shares responsibility with the Walter Library for reference services to undergraduate liberal arts students.

[12]Respondent's answers apply to seven subject areas in the main library and to a small general reference unit which is staffed nights and weekends when subject area desks are generally not staffed. The general reference unit also has a bibliographer for International Studies and has responsibility for a current periodicals room.

[13]The main library at New York University has the following service points general reference/humanities, catalog information desk, social science, science, music, and instructional media. There is also a business branch and autonomous medical and law libraries. The personnel figures reported here are for the combined general reference/humanities and catalog information desk staffs. Reference staff work at the catalog information desk.

[14]Includes .25 volunteer librarians.

[15]The responses are for the Alexander Library for Social Sciences and Humanities. There are two research library reference departments. The second is the Library of Science and Medicine which is located on a different campus.

[16]The responses as for the Lockwood Library which is the graduate library for the social sciences and the humanities.  The Library system includes seven other units:  Undergraduate Library, Science and Engineering, Health Sciences, Law, Poetry/Archives/Special Collections.

[17]At Temple general reference service is provided at two desks.  The Information Desk has the longest hours and provides all types of general reference service.  During peak hours (11 a.m.-3 p.m.) a small reference desk provides help with questions requiring extended advice or teaching and the Information Desk handles only ready reference.  There is also a catalog information desk which is open from 11 a.m.-3 p.m. and which is organizationally under Technical Services, although it is staffed in part by reference librarians.

[18]Vanderbilt was in a transition phase when the questionnaire was filled out.  They were in the process of integrating into a centralized unit eleven librarians who were offering service in four locations.  The questionnaire was answered as though the integration of Central Reference, Science Reference, Documents and Arts had already taken place.

Table 2.  Distribution of Responsibility for Reference Services by Subject within Libraries (Percent of Respondents, N=65)

| Unit(s) Responsible[1] | Subject Area | | | | | | | | | | | | | | | | |
|---|---|---|---|---|---|---|---|---|---|---|---|---|---|---|---|---|---|
| | Humanities | Art/Architecture | Music | Soc. Sciences | Education | Business | Biological Sciences | Physical Sciences | Engineering | Medicine | Law | Government | Maps | Microforms | Rare Bks. | Local History | Av/Media |
| R | 65 | 17 | 18 | 54 | 42 | 40 | 17 | 15 | 18 | 9 | 15 | 17 | 22 | 12 | 3 | 28 | 2 |
| RB | 31 | 17 | 6 | 34 | 23 | 12 | 9 | 2 | 2 | 2 | 2 | 15 | 8 | 20 | 2 | 12 | 2 |
| BR | 2 | 62 | 68 | 11 | 29 | 40 | 57 | 69 | 63 | 40 | 23 | 29 | 35 | 14 | 31 | 13 | 25 |
| B | | | | | | | 5 | 3 | 3 | 3 | 3 | 2 | 2 | 23 | 23 | 2 | 5 |
| L | 5 | 3 | 3 | | 2 | | 9 | 8 | 8 | 5 | 5 | 32 | 28 | 54 | 58 | 29 | 37 |
| O | 2 | 5 | 5 | 3 | 3 | 3 | | | 11 | 34 | 46 | | 3 | 2 | 2 | 3 | 23 |

[1] Respondents answered with codes defined as follows:  R indicates the activity is "solely the responsibility of the reference department"; RB indicates "the reference department has substantial responsibility, but the activity also goes on in branch or departmental libraries;" BR indicates that the "activity goes on primarily in the branches with back-up from the reference department; B is a code supplied by respondents to indicate that branch or departmental libraries have sole responsibility; L indicates that the activity is the responsibility of some other unit of the central library which is neither the reference department nor a branch or departmental library, and O indicates that the activity is the responsibility of agencies not under library jurisdiction, such as autonomous libraries or reading rooms in academic departments.

Summary 1.  Percentage of Reference Departments Performing Various Functions

Online Services
      96.9%

Orientation Activities
      93.70%

Interlibrary Borrowing and Lending
      Ongoing request processing                          40.6%
      Verification of Outgoing requests                   46%
      Processing of Incoming requests                     39%
      Verification of Incoming requests                   39%
      Photoduplication for Incoming Requests              25%
      Administration of the Interlibrary Loan function    48%

Physical Maintenance of a Separate Microform Collection
      18.8%

Physical Maintenance of a Separate Audio-visual Collection
      0

Physical Maintenance of a Separate Newspaper Collection
      10.9%

Processing and Maintenance of a Separate Government Documents Collection
      21.9%

(A few respondents may have interpreted this to mean simply maintenance
of whatever uncataloged documents are housed in reference, rather than
maintenance and processing for the depository collection.)

Provision of documents reference service at a point separate from the
      main reference desk
      29.6%

Preparation of Bibliographies
      81.3%

Selection for the General Collections and Liaison Work with Teaching
      Departments
      67.1%

Preparation of Exhibits
      62.5%

      Responses indicate that the preparation of exhibits is usually a
professional activity, but rarely occupies any substantial amount of
professional time.

Vertical File Maintenance
      59.3%

Maintenance of a Thesis Catalog or List
      35.9%

Table 3. Estimates of Staff (in FTEs) Allocated to Major Functions in Reference Departments Surveyed*

| Institution | Online Searching[1] | | Instruction** | | | | Interlibrary Loan | | | | Govt. Docs. Processing | | | Separate Doc. Ref. | | | General Collection Dev.[2] | | | Library Comm. Work[3] | Microform Collection | | |
| --- | --- | --- | --- | --- | --- | --- | --- | --- | --- | --- | --- | --- | --- | --- | --- | --- | --- | --- | --- | --- | --- | --- | --- |
| | P | C | P | C | SA | PP | P | C | SA | PP | P | C | SA | P | C | SA | P | C | SA | PP | P | C | SA |
| Arizona[4] | .50 | | .60 | .15 | | | | 3.00 | | | | | | | | | .20 | | | .10 | | | |
| Ariz. State[5] | 1.50 | .25 | 2.38 | | | | | | | | | | | | | | 4.5 | | | 1.5 | | | |
| BYU[6] | .05 | | .40 | .30 | | 1.5 | .25 | 2.00 | 2.75 | | | | | | | | .3 | | | .50 | | | |
| UCLA | .23 | | .21 | | | | 1.00 | 1.08 | .88 | | | | | | | | | | | .45 | | | |
| San Diego | .10 | | - | | .35 | | .43 | 6.50 | | | | | | | | | .7 | | | 2.0 | | | |
| S. Bar.[7] | - | - | - | | | | | 4.95 | .75 | | | | | | | | | | | - | | | |
| Chicago | .20 | | .16 | | | | 1.05 | 1.00 | 1.10 | .05 | | .75[8] | | | | | .05 | | | .30 | | | |
| Cinn. | .50 | | .75 | 2.00 | | | | | | | 1.0 | 2.0 | 1.5 | | | | 5.0 | 1.0 | .10 | .25 | | | |
| Colo. | .38 | .25 | 2.0 | .13 | | | | | | | | | | | | | 3.25 | | | 1.00 | | | |
| Columbia | .40 | | | | | | | | | | | | | | | | | | | - | | | |
| Conn. | .75 | | 1.00 | | | | .10 | | | | | | | | | | | | | .30 | | | |
| Cornell | .25 | | .15 | .05 | | | | | | | | | | | | | | | | .60 | | | |
| Florida[9] | 1.00 | .13 | 3.85 | .50 | .25 | | .85 | 2.0 | 1.75 | | | | | .50 | 1.00 | | 2.00 | .30 | .50 | 2.00 | | | |
| G'town[10] | .10 | | .36 | | | | | 1.0 | 2.0 | | 1.0 | 1.0 | 2.0 | .80 | .50 | | | | | .05 | | | |
| Ga. Tech[11] | .26 | | | | | | | | | | | | | | | | | | | .08 | | | |
| Hawaii[12] | .50 | .10 | 1.05 | .30 | | | | | | | | | | | | | 3.00 | | .25 | .50 | | | |
| Houston[13] | 3.00 | .50 | 4.0 | .50 | .25 | | | 2.50 | 1.00 | | .50 | 1.75 | 2.25 | | | | 4.00 | 2.0 | 2.0 | .25 | | | |
| Illinois[14] | .38 | .05 | .20 | .15 | | | .80 | 2.00 | 1.00 | | | | | | | | | | | .10 | | | |
| Indiana | 1.30 | .40 | .75 | | | | | 2.00 | 1.00 | | | | | | | | | | | 1.25 | | | |
| Iowa[15] | 1.0 | | 1.30 | .50 | | | 2.35 | 2.50 | 1.00 | | | | | | | | | | | 1.00 | | | |
| J. Hop. | .75 | | .30 | .50 | | | | | | | | | | | | | .50 | | | .10 | | | |
| Kansas[16] | .50 | | .50 | | | | 1.00 | 4.00 | 3.03 | .40 | 2.0[17] | 3.0[17] | | | | | 4.00 | | .5 | 1.00 | | 1.00 | |
| Kentucky | .30 | | .27 | .20 | | .02 | .60 | | | | | | | | | | | | | .05 | | | |
| LSU | 1.10 | .40 | 1.30 | .20 | | .03 | .20 | 1.00 | | | .05 | | | | | | | | | .10 | | | |
| Manitoba[18] | .80 | .04 | .63 | .04 | | | .20 | 3.10 | | | | 1.2 | | .25 | .75 | | 3.6 | | | 1.00 | | | 1.0 |

Table 3. (cont'd.)

| Institution | Online Searching[1] P | C | Instruction** P | C | SA | PP | Interlibrary Loan P | PP | C | SA | Govt. Docs. Proc. P | C | SA | Separate Doc. Ref. P | C | SA | Gen. Collection Dev.[2] P | C | SA | Library Comm. Work P | Microform Collection P | C | SA |
|---|---|---|---|---|---|---|---|---|---|---|---|---|---|---|---|---|---|---|---|---|---|---|---|
| Mass. | .75 | .15 | .28 | .2 | | | | | | | | | | | | | .40 | | | .10 | .50 | 1.00 | 1.60 |
| Mich. St. | .33 | | 2.25 | .05 | | | | | 1.00 | 4.00 | .25 | 1.0 | 1.0 | .50 | 1.0 | .25 | .25 | | | 2.00 | | | |
| Minn. | .75 | .50 | 1.00 | .05 | | | | | | | | | | | | | | | | .10 | | 1.00 | |
| N. Mexico | 1.00 | .50 | 1.00 | .07 | .50 | | | | | | | | | | | | 1.50 | | | - | 1.00 | | |
| NYU | .10 | .50 | .14 | .07 | | | .04 | | 1.40 | .10 | | | | .10 | .90 | | 1.50 | | | .02 | | | |
| N. Car. St. | .63 | .13 | .33 | .12 | | | | | | | | | | | | | .15 | .03 | | .60 | | | |
| Northwestern | 1.75 | .15 | 2.90 | .35 | | | .25 | | 2.80 | | | | | | .10 | | | | | 1.50 | | | |
| Notre D. | 1.00 | | 1.80 | .35 | | | | | | | .90 | 1.85 | .5 | | | | .50 | | | .75 | | .50 | .50 |
| Okla. | .50 | | 1.70 | | | | | | | | 1.0[17] | 3.0[17] | 1.5[17] | | | | 4.00 | | | .20 | | | |
| Oregon | .90 | | 2.33 | 1.01 | | | 2.37 | | .62 | 2.26 | .24 | .9 | | 1.2 | .63 | .25 | 2.00 | | | .90 | | | |
| Penn.[19] | .30 | | 1.68 | | | | | | | | | | | | | | | | | .25 | | | |
| Penn. St. | 1.5 | .10 | 1.3 | .10 | .25 | | | | | | | | | | | | .10 | | | .20 | | | |
| Pitt. | 1.75 | .37 | .25 | .25 | | | .50 | | | | | | | | | | .50 | | | | | | |
| Rice | .20 | | .40 | | | | | | | | | | | | | | 4.00 | | | | | | |
| SUNY-Buf.[20] | 1.00 | .10 | 1.28 | .10 | | | | | | | | | | | | | | | | .15 | | | |
| SUNY-St.Br.[21] | 1.00 | | .50 | | | | .58 | | .90 | .50 | 2.0 | 1.75 | | 2.0 | .25 | .50 | .50 | | | .30 | | .50 | |
| Temple | .50 | | 1.34 | | | | .75 | | 2.70 | | 1.33 | 3.0 | | 2.9 | .33 | | 3.80 | | | .75 | | 1.00 | |
| Tenn. | 1.60 | .05 | .27 | .07 | | | | | | | .75 | .25 | | .75 | .25 | | | | | .10 | | | |
| Texas[22] | 1.90 | | 1.25 | .07 | .20 | .125 | | | | | .13 | 2.70 | .35 | | | | .60 | .125 | 2.0 | .46 | | 1.00 | 2.00 |
| Tex A&M | 3.00 | 1.00 | 3.10 | | | | 1.00 | | 1.00 | | | .60 | | | | | 2.10 | | | 2.00 | | .90 | 2.85 |
| Tulane[23] | .10 | | .14 | .07 | | | 1.00 | | 1.00 | | | | | .40 | | | .40 | .50 | 2.0 | .10 | | .85 | .15 |
| Van'bilt | .35 | | 2.25 | .55 | .30 | | | | | | | | | | 1.0 | .50 | 3.50 | 1.00 | | .50 | | | |
| Wash.[24] | .80 | .13 | .08 | .07 | | | | | | | | | | .43 | .56 | | 1.25 | .15 | | .30 | | .25 | |
| Wisc. | .75 | .13 | 1.75 | .125 | | | | | | | .75 | | | | | | | | | | | .25 | 1.20 |
| Yale[25] | .25 | | 2.20 | | | | | | 3.6 | .50 | | | | | | | | | | .20 | .50 | 1.50 | .80 |

*Not all institutions surveyed could supply staff allocation estimates. Figures tabulated are for those functions requiring significant amounts of staff time but which are not part of the provision reference desk services.

General Explanation of terms: Instruction includes all staff designated as allocated to instruction as well as orientation activities, preparation of bibliographies and preparation of general guides and user aids. The designations "P" "C", "SA" and "PP" in the column headings stand for professional staff (P), clerical staff (C) (all levels of support staff including paraprofessionals), student assistants (SA) and preprofessional staff (PP) (i.e., library school students, if applicable).

1.  In the interest of simplifying the display of figures in this table, allocations of student assistant or pre-professional staff are shown only when a fairly large number of departments employ this level of staff for the function in question. Footnotes will indicate their use in other functions for the few departments where they play a role. In the case of online searching, Brigham Young University allocates .15 FTE preprofessionals to the activity and Vanderbilt allocates .05 FTE. Colorado, Connecticut, New Mexico, and SUNY-Buffalo employ, respectively, .25 FTE, .10 FTE, .25 FTE and .10 FTE student assistants in online searching activities.

2.  Vanderbilt University employs .10 FTE preprofessional to assist with development of the general collections and the University of Washington employs .05 FTE.

3.  Librarians in a few reference departments require mostly small amounts of clerical support for their work on library committees. Allocations listed are: UCLA (.01 FTE), Cincinnati (.10 FTE), Florida (.10 FTE), Indiana (.10 FTE), Louisiana State (.01 FTE), Manitoba (.02 FTE), Notre Dame (.05 FTE), Oklahoma (.10 FTE), Tennessee (.02 FTE) and Texas A & M (.40 FTE).

4.  .25 FTE professional staff are devoted to faculty liaison activities.

5.  .75 FTE in professional time is for professional development, publication, etc. 1.25 FTE in professional time is allocated to "projects" and departmental governance.

6.  .40 FTE in professional time is spent in professional development. .55 FTE clerical support is for secretarial work.

7.  1.0 FTE professional is the Black Studies Librarian who has a support staff of 1.0 FTE clerical and 1.0 FTE in student assistants. Also 1.0 FTE is the Chicano Studies Librarian who has a support staff of 1.0 FTE clerical and 1.38 FTE student assistants. Part of the time of an additional professional, 1.0 FTE clerical and .25 student assistant are devoted to the Curriculum Laboratory. Information Desk/Microcopy/Special Service Center requires 1.0 FTE clerical staff, 3.5 FTE student assistants.

8.  Not for maintenance of the depository collection, but only for those uncataloged documents located in reference.

9.  Maintenance of the U.S. census tape access program at Florida requires .75 FTE professionals, .15 FTE clerical staff, and .50 FTE student assistants. Urban documents collection maintenance requires .50 FTE professionals and .30 FTE student assistants. The Map Library requires an additional 1.0 FTE professionals, 1.0 FTE clerical staff and 1.0 FTE student assistants.

10. Production of the faculty publications list, coordination of library services for the handicapped, assignment of library studies requires .35 FTE in clerical time.

11. .15 FTE clerk is required for indexing school and local newspapers.

12. .10 FTE clerk is required to maintain RAND and ERIC reports collection.

13. Support of the branches under reference department supervision requires 1.75 FTE professionals, 8.0 FTE clerks and 3.0 FTE student assistants. An additional .10 FTE professional and .25 FTE clerks are devoted to the Map collection. Houston's reference department also maintains the Library Copy Center which requires .25 FTE professionals, 3.0 FTE clerical staff and 2.0 FTE student assistants. 1.5 clerical staff forms the office typing pool.

14. At Illinois .50 FTE professionals are required to supervise the Information Desk, .25 FTE clerical staff work at the desk as well as 2.25 FTE pre-professional staff and 1.1 FTE student assistants.

15. .20 clerical staff at Iowa are required to file cards in the Undergraduate Library; .30 professionals are required to order books for the Undergraduate Library.

16. At Kansas, interlibrary loan is handled by a separate department which reports to the head of Reference. Its total staff complement is 1.0 FTE professional and 4.0 FTE clerical.

17. The combined staff needed for both documents processing and reference from a separate service point.

18. 1.6 FTE professionals are involved in supervision of Reference, Government Publications and Collection Development.

19. Physical maintenance of a separate newspaper collection at Pennsylvania requires .25 FTE clerks and .50 FTE student assistants.

20. .30 FTE professionals are required for the training of preprofessionals and for the supervision of practicums for library school students.

21. .50 FTE professionals are needed for the Map section as well as .50 FTE student assistants.

22. Physical maintenance of a central newspaper collection at Texas requires .25 FTE clerks and .20 FTE student assistants.

23. Physical maintenance of a central newspaper collection at Tulane requires .50 FTE clerks.

24. Physical maintenance of a central newspaper collection at Washington requires .25 FTE clerks and 1.5 student assistants.

25. .80 FTE professional is responsible for the Map collection, along with 1.0 FTE clerical staff member and .4 FTE student assistants. .50 FTE professional, 1.0 FTE clerical staff and .8 student assistant are responsible for the maintenance of a periodical room. .10 professional is responsible for the Publications Office.

Table 4.  Adjusted Reference Staff Size:  Hours of Professional Service
Provided, Reference Questions Answered, Library System Type, Existence
of Undergraduate Library, Existence of Information Desk, Volumes in Library,
Campus Enrollment

| Ref.Depts. in Rank Order by Size of Professional Staff | Prof. Staff Size (FTE)[1] | Hours of Prof. Service/ Week | 1981/ 82 HEGIS data refer. trans.[2] | Libr. System type[3] | Exist. of Under grad. Libr. | Exist. of Infor mation Desk | Volumes in Library FY83[4] | Campus Enrollment Fall 1982[5] |
|---|---|---|---|---|---|---|---|---|
| Texas A & M | 12.6 | 196.00 | ---- | 1 | --- | --- | 1,418,345 | 36,127 |
| New Mexico | 11.0 | --- | --- | 2 | --- | --- | 1,126,047 | 24,056 |
| Michigan State | 10.82 | --- | --- | 3 | --- | Y | 2,898,698 | 42,730 |
| Pennsylvania | 10.4 | 143.25 | ---- | 3 | --- | --- | 3,120,176 | 22,317 |
| Penn. State | 10.0 | 133.00 | ---- | 3 | --- | Y | 2,402,938 | 36,162 |
| Tennessee | 9.9 | 185.00 | 1,595 | 2 | --- | --- | 1,448,738 | 27,041 |
| Arizona | 9.8 | ---- | --- | 2 | --- | --- | 2,853,707 | 30,669 |
| Massachusetts | 9.6 | 122.5 | ---- | 2 | --- | Y | 1,938,833 | 26,517 |
| Arizona State | 9.5 | 170.00 | 4,010 | 2 | --- | Y | 1,830,329 | 39,287 |
| UCLA | 9.0 | 121.00 | ---- | 3 | Y | Y | 5,744,144 | 34,568 |
| Oklahoma | 9.0 | 119.00 | ---- | 3 | --- | --- | 1,981,440 | 21,802 |
| Florida | 8.9 | 139.00 | 3,525 | 3 | --- | Y | 2,349,473 | 34,252 |
| UC San Diego | 8.82 | 112.00 | 3,936 | 3 | --- | --- | 1,566,293 | 13,102 |
| La.State U. | 8.4 | 126.00 | 3,260 | 2 | --- | --- | 2,017,365 | 31,100 |
| Iowa | 8.15 | 146.00 | 788 | 3 | --- | --- | 2,494,680 | 28,948 |
| UC Santa Barbara | 8.0 | 116.000 | ---- | 1 | --- | Y | 1,532,918 | 16,158 |
| Connecticut | 7.9 | 105.00 | ---- | 2 | --- | Y | 1,801,211 | 22,800 |
| Houston | 7.9 | 155.00 | ---- | 2 | Y | --- | 1,360,084 | 30,544 |
| Texas | 7.77 | 160.00 | 13,037 | 3 | --- | Y | 5,057,649 | 48,039 |
| Oregon | 7.56 | 149.50 | 800 | 3 | --- | --- | 1,566,877 | 15,405 |
| Northwestern | 7.5 | 96.00 | 900 | 2 | --- | --- | 2,973,100 | 15,703 |
| Manitoba | 7.25 | 100.00 | ---- | 3 | --- | --- | 1,293,852 | 21,293 |
| Georgia Tech. | 7.0 | 108.00 | 1,576 | 2 | --- | --- | 1,661,559 | 11,377 |
| SUNY-Stonybr. | 7.0 | 109.50 | 1,750 | 2 | --- | --- | 1,374,100 | 14,741 |
| Illinois | 6.5 | 108.00 | ---- | 2 | Y | Y | 6,411,948 | 34,914 |
| NYU | 6.46 | 98.00 | 630 | 3 | --- | Y | 2,756,470 | 32,460 |
| Columbia | 6.0 | 112.00 | 3,905 | 3 | Y | --- | 5,270,432 | 16,091 |
| Indiana | 6.0 | 95.00 | 2,647 | 3 | Y | --- | 4,105,734 | 32,711 |
| Kentucky | 6.0 | 280.00 | 1,169 | 4 | --- | --- | 1,894,632 | 22,267 |
| N. Carolina | 5.85 | 65.00 | 2,924 | 2 | --- | --- | 2,952,859 | 22,071 |
| Colorado | 5.75 | 113.00 | ---- | 3 | --- | --- | 1,972,172 | 22,177 |
| Yale | 5.5 | 100.50 | ---- | 3 | Y | --- | 7,880,025 | 10,332 |
| SUNY-Buffalo | 5.47 | 74.00 | 683 | 2[6] | Y | --- | 2,181,241 | 11,430 |
| Hawaii | 5.0 | 93.00 | ---- | 3 | Y | --- | 1,914,846 | 20,880 |
| Wisconsin | 5.0 | 67.75 | ---- | 3 | Y | --- | 4,281,749 | 42,230 |
| Chicago | 4.9 | 140.00 | 1,700 | 3 | Y | Y | 4,688,361 | 9,013 |
| Minnesota | 4.8 | 100.50 | ---- | 3[7] | --- | --- | 4,037,478 | 64,515 |
| Cincinnati | 4.75 | 128.00 | ---- | 3 | --- | Y | 1,371,023 | 32,905 |

Table 4 (cont.)

| Ref.Depts. in Rank Order by Size of Professional Staff | Prof. Staff Size[1] (FTE) | Hours of Prof. Service/ Week | 1981/ 82 HEGIS data refer. trans.[2] | Libr. System type[3] | Exist. of Under grad. Libr. | Exist. of Infor mation Desk | Volumes in Library FY83[4] | Campus Enrol- lment Fall 1982[5] |
|---|---|---|---|---|---|---|---|---|
| Notre Dame | 4.75 | 75.00 | ---- | 3 | ---- | ---- | 1,543,952 | 9,298 |
| Georgetown | 4.6 | 72.50 | ---- | 2 | ---- | ---- | 1,407,270 | 12,020 |
| Rice | 2.0 | 57.50 | ---- | 1 | ---- | ---- | 1,146,577 | 3,881 |
| Washington | 1.97 | 99.00 | 12,493 | 3 | Y | Y | 4,168,079 | 34,468 |

Footnotes to Table 11

[1]The professional staff size shown in this table is adjusted to take into account non-typical functions performed by different reference departments. Professional staff commitments to the following have been subtracted when they were indicated: interlibrary lending and borrowing, maintenance of separate microform, newspaper, audiovisual or documents collections, reference service provided at separate service points (e.g., documents, business), general collection development, branch supervision and other tasks. The number of FTE librarians in the second column of this table is therefore the number employed in performing the functions that all reference departments do, including instruction and online searching. Departments, of course, have different levels of commitment to both instruction and online searching so that even the staffing levels shown in this table are not entirely suitable for direct comparison with one another.

[2]Participants were asked to supply statistics on the number of reference transactions which took place in their departments during the academic year 1981/82. They were specifically requested to provide the figure on total reference transactions per typical week they reported to the 1981/82 Higher Education General Information/Library General Information Survey Conducted by the National Center for Education Statistics. Locally compiled annual statistics were also requested as alternative to the standard national reporting measure, but because of their lack of comparability these data are not presented in this Table.

[3]On this table library system type is derived from how libraries responded to the first question concerning the type of library system of which they are a part. Type 1 libraries are those in systems having few, if any, branches, and in which the central reference department provides essentially all the reference service to campus users. Type 2 libraries are those in systems having some branches, but where the central reference department still plays a major role in the provision of reference service to the campus community. Type 3 libraries are systems which have many branches, but where the central reference department still plays a major role in the provision of reference service to the campus community. Type 4 libraries are in systems where there

Table 4 (cont.)

are many branches and the central reference department views itself as playing a minor role in the provision of reference service to the user community.

[4]The number of volumes in the libraries were obtained from ARL Statistics, 1982-83. (Washington:  Association of Research Libraries, 1984).

[5]The figures in American university enrollment were obtained from U.S. National Center for Education Statistics Education Directory:  Colleges and Universities, 1983-84 (Washington:  United States Government Printing Office, 1984 1984).  Enrollment at the University of Manitoba was obtained from the Commonwealth Universities Yearbook.  (London:  The Association of Commonwealth Universities, 1984).

[6]SUNY-Buffalo will be treated as a type 2 library since it is part of a system which consists of seven units one of which is an undergraduate library.

[7]Since responses to the questionnaire are for the Wilson Library (which is the main library for the social sciences and the humanities) and since the Library system consists of 5 major libraries plus branches, for the purpose of comparison, Minnesota will be treated as a type 3 library.

57

Table 5.  Professional and Non-Professional Service Provided in Research
Library Reference Departments 1982/83

| Institution | # of FTE Ref. Librs. | Aver. Desk/ Hours/ Week/ Librn. | No.of Hrs. dur. which Prof. Ref. Serv. is Prov. Ea/wk. | Librn Hrs. Ref. Serv. Ea/Wk | Total Ref. Serv. Hrs./ Week | % of Ref. Serv Prov. by Profs. | Open Hrs./ Week | % of Bldg. Hrs. Prof. Ref. Serv. Prov. |
|---|---|---|---|---|---|---|---|---|
| Alabama | 7.00 | 14 | 74 | 94 | 103 | 79.0 | 92 | 80 |
| Arizona | 10.00 | 13 | | | 229 | | 118 | |
| Arizona St. | 14.00 | 12 | 81 | 170 | 170 | 100 | 105 | 77 |
| BYU | 3.00 | 13 | 42 | 42 | 146 | 29 | 95 | 44 |
| Brown | 11.00 | 10 | 61 | | 85 | | 100.5 | 59 |
| Calif.-Berkeley | 11.50 | 12 | 77 | 167 | 172 | 97 | 82 | 94 |
| Calif.-Irvine | 7.00 | 9 | 73 | 60 | | | 89 | 82 |
| UCLA | 10.00 | 15 | 82 | 121 | 170 | 71 | 87 | 94 |
| Cal.-San Diego | 9.95 | 11 | 82 | 112 | 112 | 100 | 93 | 88 |
| Cal.-Santa Barb. | 10.00 | 16 | 81 | 116 | 116 | 100 | 103 | 79 |
| Case Western | 3.00 | | 75 | 97 | 97 | 100 | 103 | 73 |
| Chicago | 6.00 | 33.5[2] | 64.5 | 140 | 140 | 100 | 106 | 61 |
| Cincinnati | 10.75 | 10 | 64 | 128 | 128 | 100 | 100 | 64 |
| Colorado | 9.00 | 13 | 78 | 113 | 127 | 89 | 107 | 73 |
| Columbia | 6.00 | 10 | 67 | 112 | 136 | 82 | 79 | 85 |
| Connecticut | 8.00 | 12 | 70 | 105 | 105 | 100 | 96 | 73 |
| Cornell | 7.00 | 12 | 60 | 93 | 93 | 100 | 94 | 64 |
| Delaware | 15.75 | 12 | 72 | 104 | 104 | 100 | 106.5 | 68 |
| Duke | 6.75 | 14.5 | 83.5 | 107.5 | 133.5 | 81 | 99 | 84 |
| Florida[3] | 14.50 | 14 | 73.5 | 139 | 139 | 100 | 106 | 69 |
| Georgetown | 6.50 | 17 | 72.5 | 115 | 129 | 89 | 98.5 | 74 |
| Georgia Tech. | 7.00 | 17 | 83 | 108 | 118 | 92 | 93 | 89 |
| Harvard | 4.00 | 28 | 73 | | | | 73 | 100 |
| Hawaii | 8.00 | 10 | 59 | 93 | 97 | 96 | 88.5 | 67 |
| Houston | 14.00 | 12 | 93 | 155 | 211 | 73 | 101.25 | 92 |
| Illinois | 7.00 | 12 | 67 | 108 | 118 | 92 | 102 | 66 |
| Indiana | 6.00 | 15 | 109 | 95 | 230 | 41 | 109 | 100 |
| Iowa | 10.50 | 15 | 82 | 146 | 146 | 100 | 123 | 67 |
| Johns Hopkins | 6.00 | 12 | 72 | 136 | 136 | 100 | 106 | 68 |
| Kansas | 8.50 | 12 | 83 | 138.5 | 138.5 | 100 | 98 | 85 |
| Kentucky | 6.00 | 12 | 88 | 280 | 334 | 84 | 104 | 85 |
| Louisiana St. | 9.00 | 15 | 89.5 | 126 | 201 | 63 | 104.75 | 85 |
| Manitoba | 11.35 | 11 | 70.5 | 100 | 100 | 100 | 78.5 | 90 |
| Massachusetts | 10.50 | 14.5 | 89.5 | 122.5 | 133 | 92 | 100 | 90 |
| Michigan St. | 12.00 | 14 | 82 | | 216 | | 113 | 73 |
| Minnesota | 5.80 | 10 | 72 | 100.5 | 160 | 63 | 122 | 59 |
| Missouri | 16.00 | 15 | 74 | | 77 | | 100.5 | 74 |

Table 5.  Professional and Non-Professional Service Provided in Research
Library Reference Departments 1982/83

| Institution | # of FTE Ref. Librs. | Aver. Desk/ Hours/ Week/ Librn. | No.of Hrs. dur. which Prof. Ref. Serv. is Prov. Ea/wk. | Librn Hrs. Ref. Serv. Ea/Wk | Total Ref. Serv. Hrs./ Week | % of Ref. Serv Prov. by Profs. | Open Hrs./ Week | % of Bldg. Hrs. Prof. Ref. Serv. Prov. |
|---|---|---|---|---|---|---|---|---|
| New Mexico | 13.00 | 14 | 80 | | 240[4] | | 103 | 78 |
| New York Univ. | 8.00 | 12 | 70 | 98 | 114[5] | 86 | 84.5 | 83 |
| North Carolina St. | 6.00 | 12 | 82.5 | 65 | 199.5 | 33 | 103.25 | 80 |
| Northwestern | 7.50 | 10 | 73.5 | 96 | 124.75 | 77 | 103.25 | 71 |
| Notre Dame | 6.50 | 10 | 90 | 75 | 135 | 56 | 104.25 | 86 |
| Oklahoma | 9.00 | 14 | 102 | 119 | 182 | 65 | 103 | 99 |
| Oregon | 11.25 | 11 | 80 | 149.5 | 160.5 | 93 | 91 | 88 |
| Pennsylvania | 10.50 | 15 | 80.25 | 143.25 | 153.25 | 93 | 94.25 | 85 |
| Penn. State | 10.50 | 13 | 84 | 133 | 169 | 79 | 103.5 | 81 |
| Pittsburgh | 8.00 | 12 | 74.75 | 69 | 69 | 100 | 111.5 | 67 |
| Queens | 4.66 | 17 | 63 | 100.5 | 100.5 | 100 | 99 | 64 |
| Rice | 6.00 | 7.7 | 57.5 | 57.5 | 57.5 | 100 | 99 | 58 |
| Rutgers | 8.00 | 15 | 98 | 119 | 233 | 51 | 98 | 100 |
| Southern Cal. | 7.00 | 14 | 75 | 103 | 121 | 85 | 93 | 81 |
| Stanford | 6.00 | [6] | 82 | 55 | 153 | 36 | 89 | 92 |
| SUNY-Buffalo | 6.30 | 18 | 64 | 74 | 74 | 100 | 91 | 70 |
| SUNY-Stony Br. | 13.25 | 10 | 74.5 | 109.5 | 128.5 | 85 | 93.5 | 80 |
| Syracuse | 10.00 | 18.5 | 86 | 152 | 152.0 | 100 | 86 | 100 |
| Temple | 11.45 | 9.33 | 73 | 120e[7] | 144[8] | 61 | 82 | 89 |
| Tennessee | 12.00 | 14.5 | 88 | 185 | 270 | 69 | 98 | 90 |
| Texas | 10.00 | 12 | 89 | 160 | 220 | 73 | 107 | 83 |
| Texas A & M | 14.00 | 25 | 90 | 196 | 486 | 40 | 106.5 | 85 |
| Tulane | 3.00 | 10 | 73.5 | 73.5 | 133 | 55 | 102.45 | 72 |
| Vanderbilt | 11.00 | 11 | 78 | | 95 | | 99 | 79 |
| Virginia | 6.00 | 16 | 60 | | 144 | | 99 | 61 |
| Washington | 4.95 | 14 | 69 | 99 | 99 | 100 | 83.5 | 83 |
| Washington St. | 10.00 | 12 | 78 | 126.5 | 126.5 | 100 | 102.5 | 76 |
| Wisconsin | 5.00 | 13 | 63.75 | 63.75 | 98.75 | 65 | 95.25 | 71 |
| Yale | 5.50 | 17.5 | 69.5 | 100.5 | 100.5 | 100 | 87.5 | 79 |
| Averages over all departments | | 13.57 | 76.73 | 111.48 | 153.36 | 80.32 | 98.81 | 81.38 |

[1]Excludes the department head
[2]Reference librarians work all the time they are not at meetings, etc.; one
librarian is full-time supervisor of interlibrary loan and the head of the
department helps out at the desk only occasionally

[3]Florida maintains 2 service points:  the Library West desk is the main point, but there is a second desk (Library East) staffed a half-time librarian.
[4]New Mexico has two reference service points staffed by two librarians during most hours.
[5]Reference service hours include hours worked by reference librarians at the catalog information desk.
[6]Stanford cannot quote an average; varies from a low of 2 to 3 hours to a high of 12 to 15.
[7]Reference librarians also staff the Business/Documents desk for 71 hours each week
[8]These are the hours provided at the general reference desks.  General reference service is divided between two desks.  The Information Desk is closest to the library entrance, has the longest hours and provides all types of general reference service except between 11 a.m. and 3 p.m.  During those peak hours there is a small reference desk open which is staffed only by librarians.

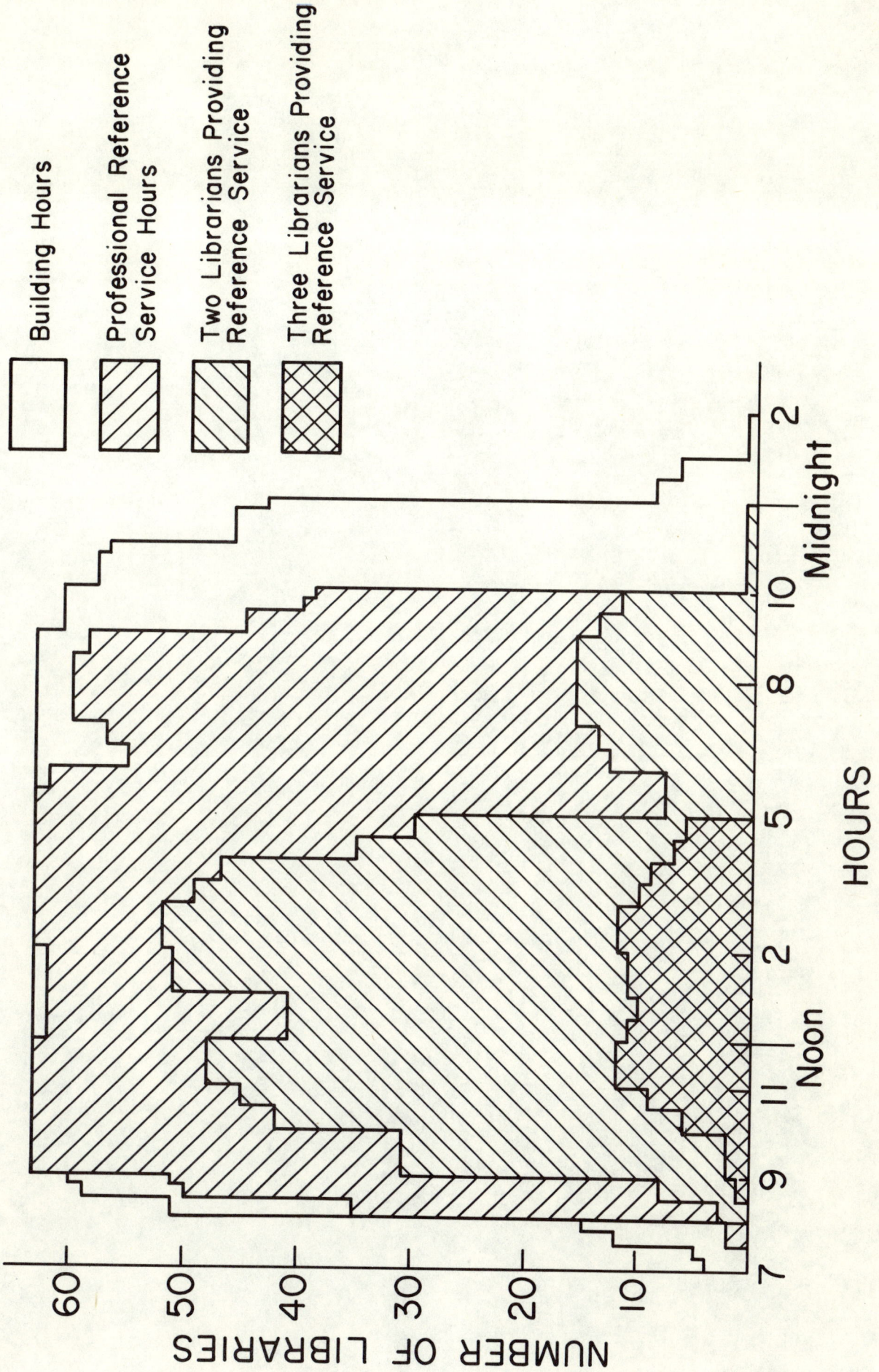

Figure 1. Reference Staffing in Relation to Building Hours, Mondays through Thursdays

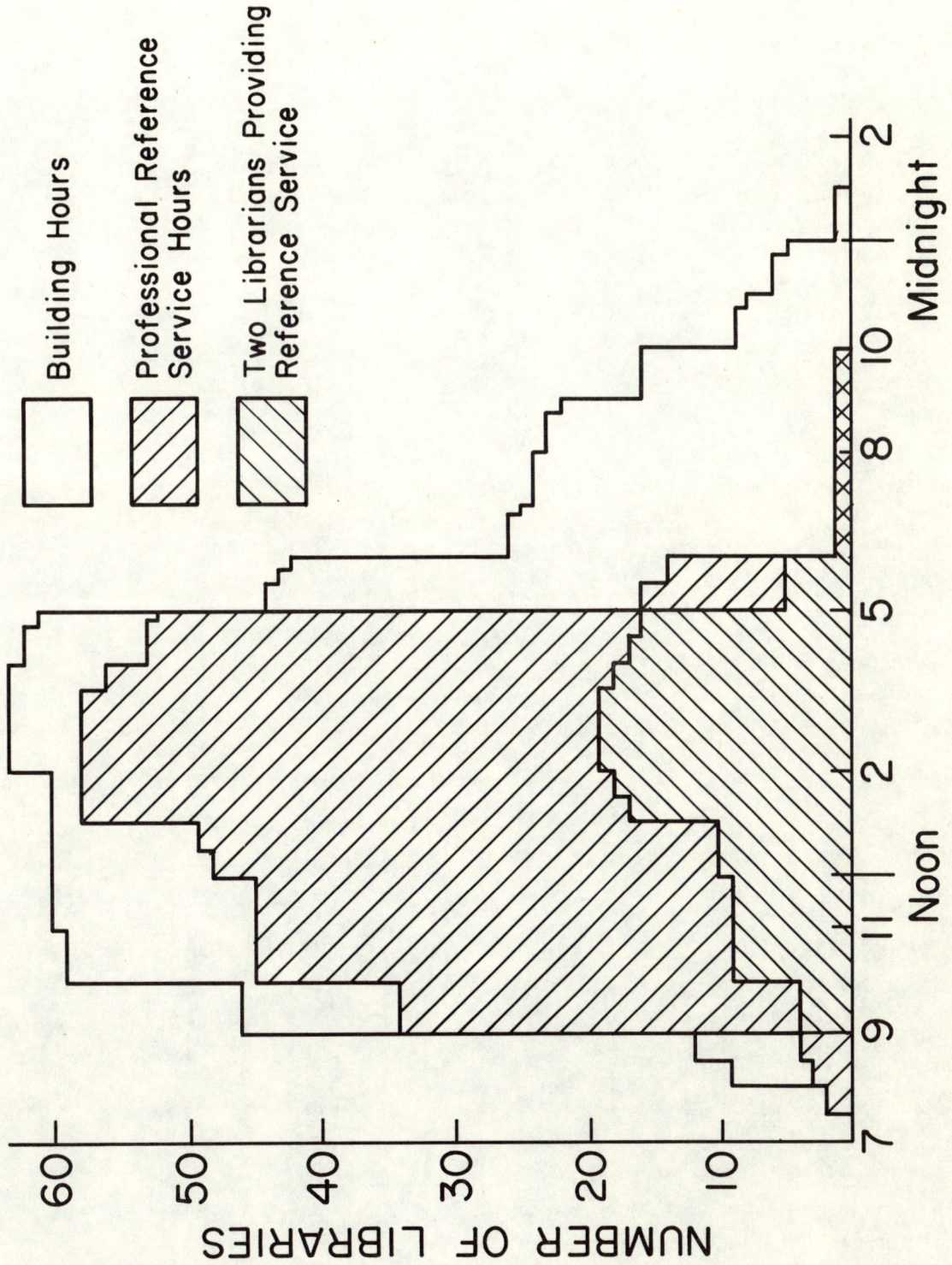

Figure 2. Reference Staffing in Relation to Building Hours, Saturdays

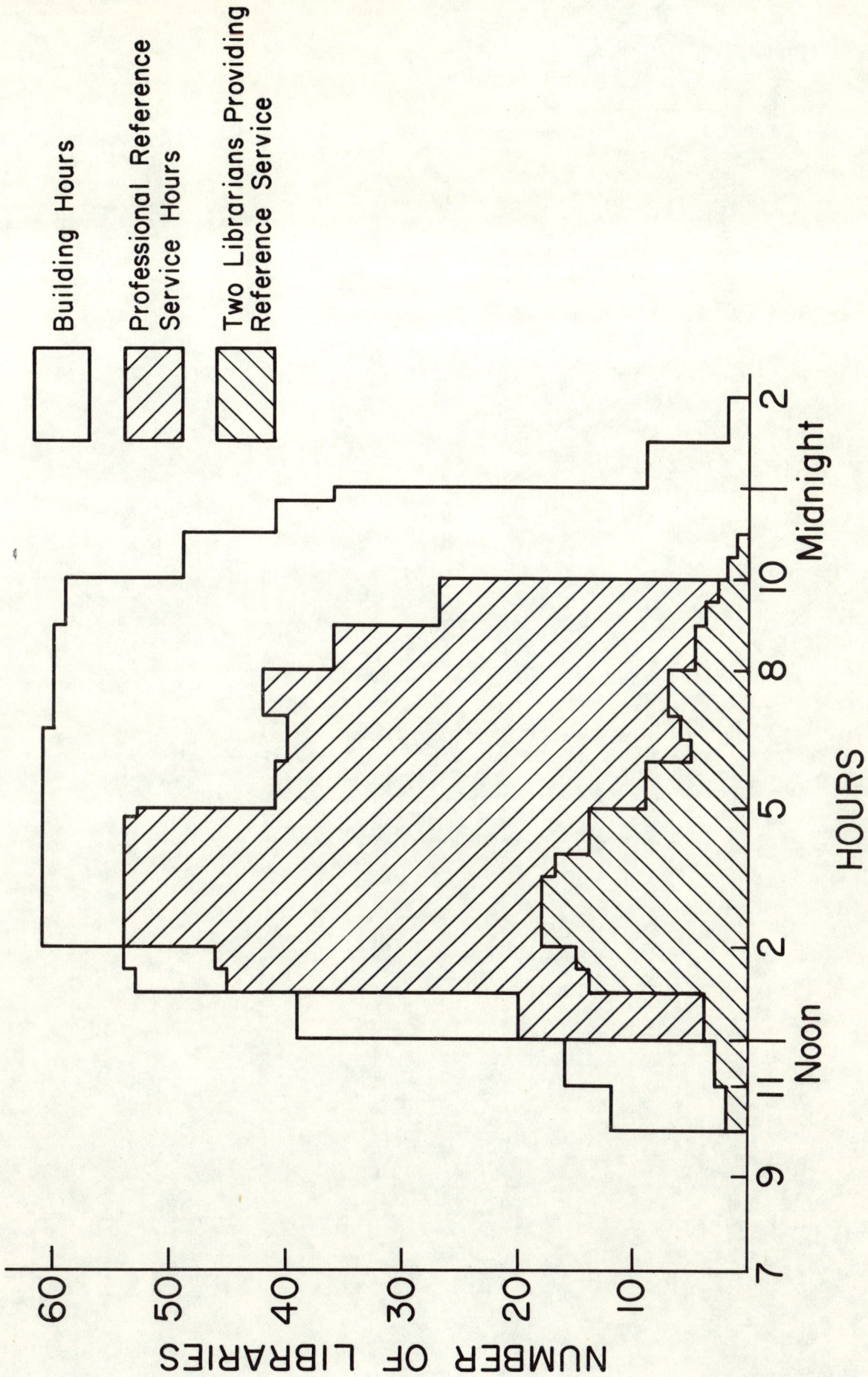

Figure 3. Reference Staffing in Relation to Building Hours, Sundays

Table 6.  Reference Productivity (Questions Answered):  1977 and 1982

| Institution | Fall 1978 HEGIS Data on Reference Trans.[1] | Spring 1982 HEGIS Data on Ref.Trans | % Change | 1977/78 Local Data on Reference Transact. | 1981/82 Local Data on Reference Transact. | % Change |
|---|---|---|---|---|---|---|
| Arizona | ---- | ---- | ---- | 118,562 | 116,322 | - 2 |
| Arizona State | ---- | 4,010 | ---- | ---- | ---- | ---- |
| Alabama | 400 | 514 | +22 | ---- | ---- | ---- |
| Brown | N.A. | 1,292 | ---- | ---- | ---- | ---- |
| UCLA | 3,757 | 2,997 | -25 | ---- | ---- | ---- |
| UC-San Diego | 3,939 | 3,936 | ---- | ---- | ---- | ---- |
| UC-Santa Bar. | ---- | ---- | ---- | 131,559 | 118,754 | ---- |
| Case Western | 400 | 500 | +20 | ---- | ---- | ---- |
| Chicago | 922 | 1,700 | +46 | ---- | ---- | ---- |
| Cincinnati | ---- | ---- | ---- | 48,799 | 67,902 | +11 |
| Colorado | ---- | ---- | ---- | 66,015 | 74,628 | +16 |
| Columbia | 5,295 | 3,905 | -36 | ---- | ---- | ---- |
| Cornell | 1,018 | ---- | ---- | 58,121 | 54,189 | - 7 |
| Delaware | ---- | ---- | ---- | ---- | 51,459 | ---- |
| Florida | N.A. | 3,525 | ---- | N.A. | 175,000 | ---- |
| Georgetown | ---- | ---- | ---- | 27,000 | 42,000 | +36 |
| Georgia Tech. | 720 | 1,576 | +54 | ---- | ---- | ---- |
| Harvard | ---- | ---- | ---- | ---- | 51,258 | ---- |
| Houston | ---- | ---- | ---- | ---- | 164,747 | ---- |
| Indiana | 1,650 | 2,647 | +38 | 1,650 | 2,647 | +38 |
| Iowa | ---- | 788 | ---- | 73,858 | 95,970 | +23 |
| Johns Hopkins | ---- | ---- | ---- | ---- | 36,000 | ---- |
| Kansas | ---- | ---- | ---- | 21,000 | 32,000 | +34 |
| Kentucky | 1,633 | 1,169 | -40 | ---- | ---- | ---- |
| LSU | ---- | 3,260 | ---- | ---- | ---- | ---- |
| Manitoba | ---- | ---- | ---- | 12,942 | 37,505 | +65 |
| Massachusetts | ---- | ---- | ---- | 91,625 | 79,971 | -15 |
| Michigan | ---- | 4,670 | ---- | ---- | 43,741 | ---- |
| Missouri | ---- | ---- | ---- | 80,000 | 101,000 | +21 |
| New Mexico | ---- | ---- | ---- | 117,556 | ---- | ---- |
| New York | 567 | 630 | +10 | ---- | ---- | ---- |
| N. Carolina | 1,919 | 2,924 | +34 | ---- | ---- | ---- |
| Northwestern | ---- | 900 | ---- | ---- | ---- | ---- |
| Notre Dame | ---- | ---- | ---- | ---- | 30,095 | ---- |
| Oregon | ---- | 800 | ---- | ---- | 17,096 | ---- |
| Penn. State | ---- | ---- | ---- | 77,000 | 77,000 | ---- |
| Pittsburgh | 73,124 | ---- | ---- | ---- | ---- | ---- |
| Queen's | ---- | ---- | ---- | 25,575 | 23,670 | - 8 |
| Rice | ---- | ---- | ---- | 22,844 | 29,458 | +22 |
| Stanford | 378 | 757 | +50 | 39,035 | 78,802 | +50 |
| SUNY-Buffalo | ---- | 683 | ---- | ---- | 36,362 | ---- |
| SUNY-Stonybr. | 1,232 | 1,175 | - 5 | ---- | ---- | ---- |

| Institution | Fall 1978 HEGIS Data on Reference Trans.[1] | Spring 1982 HEGIS Data on Ref.Trans | % Change | 1977/78 Local Data on Reference Transact. | 1981/82 Local Data on Reference Transact. | % Change |
|---|---|---|---|---|---|---|
| Syracuse | --- | 2,543 | --- | --- | --- | --- |
| Temple | 2,249 | 2,030 | - 6 | --- | --- | --- |
| Tennessee | 1,396 | 1,595 | +14 | --- | --- | --- |
| Texas | --- | 13,037 | --- | 94,387 | 110,983 | +15 |
| Texas A & M | --- | --- | --- | 89,600 | 96,000 | + 7 |
| Tulane | 1,521 | 2,400 | +37 | --- | --- | --- |
| Vanderbilt | 487 | 456 | - 7 | --- | --- | --- |
| Virginia | 4,237 | 5,148 | +18 | --- | --- | --- |
| Washington | N.A. | 12,493 | --- | --- | --- | --- |
| Wisc. Madison | | | | 68,028 | 56,410 | -21 |

[1]participants were asked to supply total reference transactions per typical week in Spring 1978 as reported to the Higher Education General Information Survey/Library General Information Survey conducted by the National Center for Education Statistics. Actually data requested in the Fall 1978 survey were for a typical week in fall, 1978. It is presumed that most departments supplied fall, 1978 data; a few supplied the spring 1979 requested by the fall 1979 HEGIS LIBGIS Survey.

Table ... Distribution of Responsibility for User Education in Research Libraries

| Activity | % of Libraries in which Primary Responsibility Rests with: | | | | | |
| --- | --- | --- | --- | --- | --- | --- |
| | Ref. Dept. or Designated Ref. Staff (R) | Instruction Librarian or section outside the Ref. Dept. (I) | Undergraduate Library (U) | Branch or Departmental Libraries (B) | Another Unit in the main Library (O) | No Unit of the Library (X) |
| General Library Tours (Campus Users)[1] | 86.4 | 7.6 | 1.5 | — | 1.5 | 1.5 |
| General Library Tours (Off-campus Users)[2] | 71.2 | 9.1 | 1.5 | — | 6.2 | 10.6 |
| Freshman Orientation[3] | 62.1 | 7.7 | 21.2[5] | 1.5 | 1.5[6] | 4.5 |
| Freshman Instruction[4] | 66.6 | 6.1 | 18.1 | 3.0 | — | 4.5 |
| Lower Division Course-related Library Skills Instruction[7] | 69.2 | 4.6 | 16.9 | 4.6 | — | 3.1 |
| Upper Division Course-related Library Skills Instruction[8] | 80.0 | 4.6 | 4.6 | 6.2 | 1.5 | 1.5 |
| Graduate Course-related Library Skills Instruction[9] | 80.3 | 6.0 | — | 7.5 | 1.5 | 3.0 |
| Faculty Orientation or Instruction[10] | 75.7 | 7.6 | — | 6.1 | 4.5 | 3.0 |
| Development of General User Aids (i.e. not for Automated Systems)[11] | 75.7 | 7.6 | 3.0 | — | 10.6 | — |
| Development of User Aids Describing Automated Library Systems[12] | 37.9 | 7.6 | — | — | 24.2 | 7.6 |
| Development of User Aids Describing Online Search Systems[13] | 83.3 | 1.5 | — | 1.5 | 7.6 | 1.5 |

[1]Respondents were asked to use the codes designated in parentheses in the column headings to indicate the level of responsibility of various units for each activity. Coding showed the reference department to be solely responsible for general tours at 55 percent of the libraries. One library did not respond.

[2]Reference has sole responsibility for tours for off-campus users at 42 percent of the responding libraries. One library did not respond.

[3]Sole responsibility for freshman orientation is in the hands of reference in 36 percent of the responding libraries. One library did not respond.

[4]Reference has sole responsibility for freshman instruction at 47 percent of the responding libraries.

[5]At Columbia the Undergraduate library coordinates freshman orientation, but there is systemwide participation in the program.

[6]At Duke freshman orientation is in the hands of a librarywide orientation committee.

[7]Sole responsibility for lower division undergraduate library instruction rests with reference at 38 percent of the responding libraries. One library gave an unusable response.

[8]One library did not answer. Responsibility for upper-division course-related undergraduate instruction rests entirely with reference in 40 percent of the libraries.

[9]One library did not answer. Reference is solely responsible for graduate course-related library skills instruction at 39 percent of the responding libraries.

[10]Two libraries did not answer. Reference has sole responsibility for faculty orientation on instruction at 38 percent of the responding libraries.

[11]Two libraries did not answer. Reference has sole responsibility for the preparation of general user aids at 36 percent of the responding libraries

[12]Almost 20 percent of the libraries responded that this question was not applicable, presumably because they had no automated system to describe or perhaps, since some who gave this answer did have automated circulation systems, because the system is self-descriptive. Two libraries gave no answer; 21 percent responded that reference had sole responsibility.

[13]One library responded that the question is not applicable and two others did not respond. Online search user aids are developed solely by reference in 50 percent of the responding libraries.

Summary 2.    Percentage of Reference Departments Employing Various

Methods to Instruct Freshmen in the Use of the Library

| | |
|---|---|
| General tour | 49% |
| Lecture during a class period | 38% |
| Use of a work book asd part of a course | 17% |
| Presentation of a workshop | 9% |
| Short course | 2% |
| Separate credit course | 17% |
| Separate non-credit course | 3% |
| Programmed instruction | 2% |
| Audiovisual program | 17% |

Summary 3.    Percentage of Reference Departments Involved in Various

Instructional Activities

| | |
|---|---|
| Development of point-of-use aid | 74% |
| Development of guides to reference depepartment collection and services | 88% |
| Semester-length course offerings in library skills | 32% |
| Short courses in library skills | 38% |
| Semester-length course offerings in the bibliography of specific descriptions or areas | 20% |
| Development of audiovisual materials | 53% |
| Development of programmed instructional materials | 14% |

Table 8.  Instructional Productivity; 1977 and 1982 Compared

| Institution | 1978/79 HEGIS Data on Group Trans. | 1981/82 HEGIS Data on Group Trans. | % Change | Local Estimate of % Changes in Instructional activity |
|---|---|---|---|---|
| Alabama | 413 | 442 | +7 | +5 |
| Brigham Young | --- | --- | --- | +75 |
| Brown | --- | 75 | --- | --- |
| UC Irvine | 1,994 | 2,266 | +12 | +1,000 |
| UCLA | 102 | 83 | -23 | --- |
| UC-San Diego | --- | 439 | --- | --- |
| UC-Santa Barbara | --- | --- | --- | +10 |
| Case Western | 680 | 800 | +15 | --- |
| Chicago | 67 | 75 | +11 | --- |
| Cincinnati | 77 | 110 | +30 | --- |
| Colorado | --- | --- | --- | +301 |
| Cornell | --- | --- | --- | +50 |
| Delaware | --- | --- | --- | +60 |
| Duke | --- | --- | --- | +50 |
| Florida | --- | 419 | --- | +15 |
| Georgetown | --- | --- | --- | --- |
| Georgia Tech | 262 | 420 | +38 | --- |
| Houston | --- | --- | --- | +50 |
| Indiana | --- | --- | --- | +30 |
| Iowa | --- | 182 | --- | +20 |
| Johns Hopkins | --- | --- | --- | --- |
| Kansas | --- | --- | --- | -50 |
| Kentucky | 388 | 314 | -24 | --- |
| Louisiana St. | --- | 138 | --- | --- |
| Manitoba | --- | --- | --- | +300 |
| Massachusetts | --- | --- | --- | -20 |
| Michigan | 124 | 174 | +29 | +29 |
| Missouri | --- | --- | --- | +95 |
| New Mexico | --- | 1,081 | --- | --- |
| New York | 21,322 | 28,619 | +25 | +20 |
| N. Carolina | 169 | 228 | +26 | --- |
| Northwestern | 26 | 39 | +33 | --- |
| Notre Dame | --- | --- | --- | +100 |
| Oregon | --- | 1,000 | --- | +15 |
| Penn. State | --- | --- | --- | 0 |
| Pittsburgh | 82,967 | --- | --- | --- |
| Queen's | --- | --- | --- | - 7.5 |
| Stanford | 75 | 74 | - 1 | --- |
| SUNY Buffalo | --- | 208 | --- | --- |
| SUNY Stonybr. | 21 | 63 | +200 | --- |
| Syracuse | 24 | 52 | +116 | --- |
| Temple | 4 | 164 | +4,000 | --- |
| Tennessee | 1,660 | 1,841 | +10 | +10 |

Table 8.  Instructional Productivity;  1977 and 1982 Compared

| Institution | 1978/79 HEGIS Data on Group Trans. | 1981/82 HEGIS Data on Group Trans. | % Change | Local Estimate of % Changes in Instructional activity |
|---|---|---|---|---|
| Texas | 423 | 424 | + <1 | --- |
| Texas A & M | --- | --- | --- | +125 |
| Tulane | 38 | --- | --- | --- |
| Vanderbilt | 66 | 66 | 0 | --- |
| Virginia | 204 | 158 | -29 | --- |
| Washington | NA | 645 | --- | --- |
| Washington St. | --- | --- | --- | +100 |
| Wisconsin | --- | --- | --- | +300 |
| Yale | --- | --- | --- | +50 |

[1]Participants were asked to supply their answer to the Higher Education General Information/Library General Information Survey for "total group transactions in 1977/78 (or earliest year reported)".  Since the HEGIS/LIBGIS survey did not request data on group transactions until Fall 1979, it is presumed that respondents have supplied their total group transactions for 1978-79 rather than 1977-78 as was requested in error by the questionnaire.  However, only Stanford, SUNY-Stonybrook, Syracuse, and Texas specify that this is what they have done.

Table 9. Online Subject Searching in Research Library Reference Departments: 1977-82.

| Institution | Searches Done | | | | | Ref.% of Total Library Search. | 5-Year % * Increase |
|---|---|---|---|---|---|---|---|
| | 1977/78 | 1978/79 | 1979/80 | 1980/81 | 1981/82 | | |
| Arizona | 155 | 359 | 491 | 815[1] | 692 | 54 | +346 |
| Arizona St. | 310 | 642 | 695 | 824[1] | 962 | 52 | +210 |
| BYU | *Reference librarians do only RLIN searching | | | | | | |
| Brown | | | | | 802 | 100 | |
| UC-Berkeley | | | 444 | 373 | 209 | 11 | [-53] |
| Calif. (Irvine) | | | | | 590 | 21e | |
| UCLA | 121 | 119 | 160 | 159 | 138 | 56 | + 14 |
| UC-San Diego | 298 | 286 | 313 | 291 | 97 | 6 | - 67 |
| Case Western | | 75 | 43 | 29 | 36 | | [-52] |
| Chicago | 15 | 62 | 70 | 79 | 106 | 5 | +606 |
| Cincinnati** | | | | | 208 | | |
| Columbia | | | | | 265 | 8 | |
| Connecticut | 135 | 115 | 170 | 200 | 110 | | - 19 |
| Cornell** | 167 | 181 | 191 | 188 | 122 | | - 27 |
| Delaware | 302 | 274 | 318 | 282 | 288 | 100 | - 5 |
| Duke[2] | | | | | | | |
| Florida[3] | 190 | 180 | 250 | 275 | 300 | 8 | + 58 |
| Geo'town** | | | | | 390 | 87 | |
| Ga. Tech. | 604 | 497 | 431 | 481 | 277 | 36 | - 54 |
| Harvard | Modest increase each year | | | | 285 | | |
| Hawaii | | | 94 | 175 | 416 | | [+343] |
| Houston | | | 766 | 2427 | 3052 | | [+298] |
| Illinois | | | | | 127 | | |
| Indiana | 128 | 126 | 309 | 406 | 406 | 44 | +217 |
| Iowa | 320 | 475 | 475 | 450 | 650 | | +103 |
| Johns Hopkins | 613 | 609 | 594 | 771 | 570 | 100 | - 7 |
| Kansas | | | 176 | 188 | 223 | 67 | [+ 27] |
| Kentucky | 279 | 296 | 360 | 477 | 512 | | + 84 |
| Louisiana St. | 245 | 646 | 765 | 831 | 858 | 82 | +250 |
| Manitoba | 69 | 134 | 188 | 240 | 332 | 32 | +381 |
| Massachusetts | 385 | 488 | 556 | 607 | | | [+58] |
| Michigan St. | 390 | 458 | 502 | 443 | 472 | 26 | +21 |
| Minnesota | Steady incr. in subj searches | | | | 300 | | |
| Missouri | | 220[4] | 368 | 470 | 514 | | [+133] |
| New Mexico | | 337[5] | 442 | 550 | 622 | 100 | [+ 84] |
| NYU | | | | | 375 | 37 | |
| N'Western | 570 | 442 | 529 | 645 | 556 | | - 2 |
| Notre Dame** | | | | 70 | 164 | 57 | |
| Oklahoma | | | | | 261 | | |
| Oregon[6] | | 543 | 851 | 668 | 777 | 94 | [+ 43] |
| Pennsylvania | 240[7] | 280[7] | 190[7] | 314[7] | 381[7] | | [+ 59] |
| Penn. State | | | 321 | 379 | 298 | 56 | [- 7] |
| Pittsburgh | 729 | 942 | 1425 | 1346 | 2087 | 82 | +186 |
| Queen's | | 388 | 315 | 355 | 295 | 59e | [- 24] |

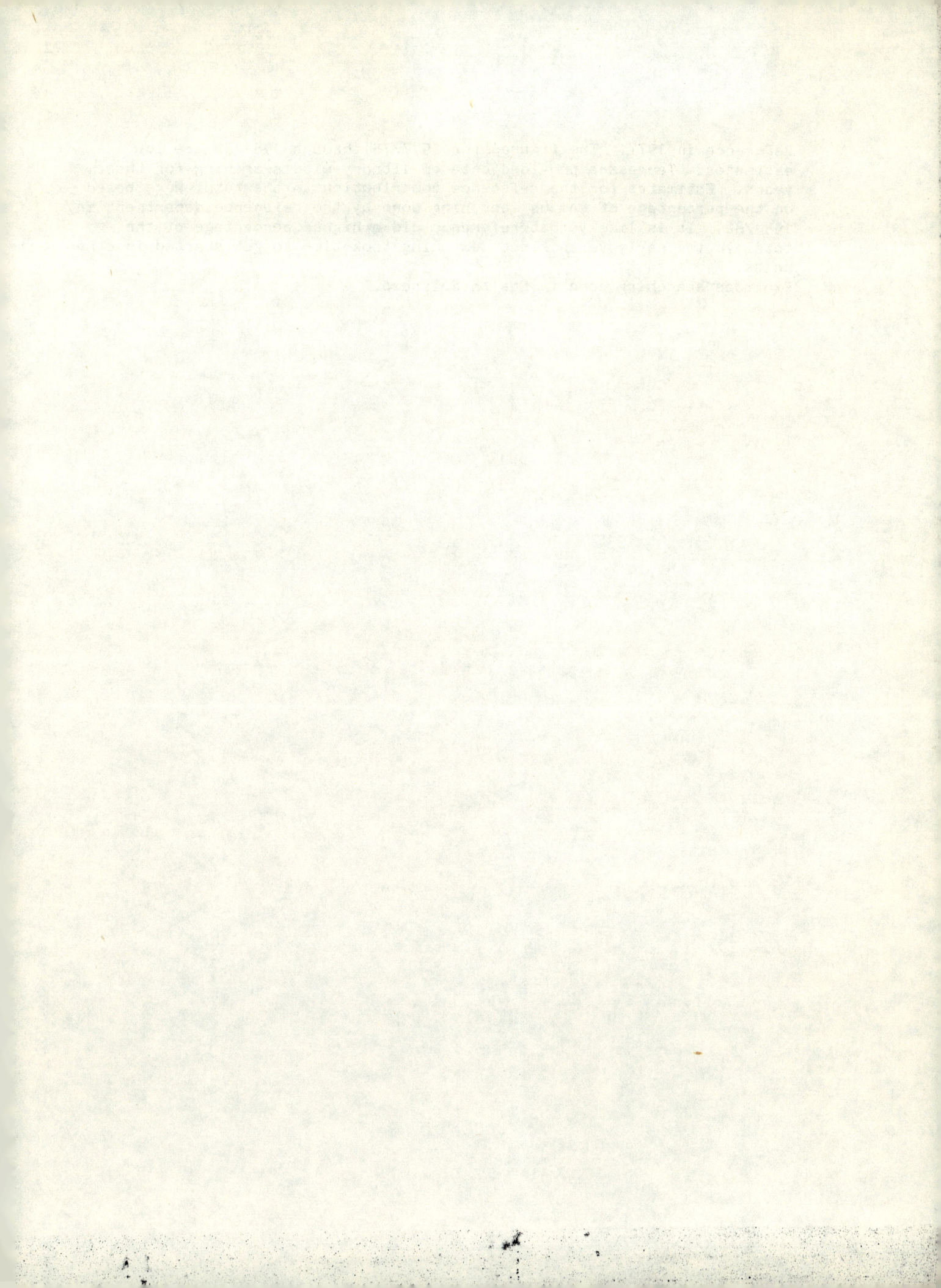

Reference in 1977.  The figures for 1977/78 through 1981/82 are low
estimates.  Tennessee provided data on library-wide searching for those
years.  Estimates for the reference contribution to the total were based
on the percentage of campus searching done by the reference department in
1981/82.  It is likely that reference did a higher percentage of the
total in the early years since searching took time to get started in other units
units.

[9]Excludes searching done in Health Sciences

Table 10.   Online Searching in Research Library Reference Departments:
            Staff Commitment and Productivity

| Institution | FTE Libr. who search | Searches Done 1981/82 | Searches/ FTE searcher |
|---|---|---|---|
| Arizona | .50 | 692 | 1384 |
| Arizona St. | 1.50 | 962 | 641 |
| BYU | | | |
| Brown | 1.60 | 802 | 501 |
| UC-Berkeley | | 209 | |
| UC-Irvine | | 590 | |
| UCLA | .23 | 138 | 613 |
| UC-San Diego | .10 | 97 | 970 |
| UC-Santa Barbara | | | |
| Case Western | | 36 | |
| Chicago | .20 | 106 | 530 |
| Cincinnati | .50 | 208 | 416 |
| Colorado | .38 | | |
| Columbia | .40 | 265 | 663 |
| Connecticut | .75 | 110 | 146 |
| Cornell | .25 | 122 | 488 |
| Delaware | | 288 | |
| Duke | | | |
| Florida | .13 | 300 | 2400 |
| Georgetown | .10 | 390 | 3900 |
| Georgia Tech. | .26 | 277 | 1065 |
| Harvard | 1.00 | 285 | 285 |
| Hawaii | .50 | 416 | 832 |
| Houston | 3.00 | 3052 | 1017 |
| Illinois | .20 | 127 | 635 |
| Indiana | 1.30 | 406 | 312 |
| Iowa | 1.00 | 650 | 650 |
| Johns Hopkins | .75 | 570 | 760 |
| Kansas | .50 | 223 | 446 |
| Kentucky | .30 | 512 | 1706 |
| Louisiana St. | 1.10 | 858 | 780 |
| Manitoba | .80 | 332e | 415e |
| Massachusetts | .75 | 706 | 941 |
| Michigan State | .33 | 472 | 1430 |
| Minnesota | .75 | 300 | 400 |
| Missouri | 1.50 | 514 | 343 |
| New Mexico | 1.00 | 622 | 622 |
| NYU | .10 | 375 | 3750 |
| No. Carolina St. | .63 | | |
| Northwestern | 1.75 | 556 | 318 |
| Notre Dame | 1.00 | 164 | 164 |
| Oklahoma | .50 | 261 | 522 |
| Oregon | .90 | 777 | 863 |

| Institution | FTE Libr. who search | Searches Done 1981/82 | Searches/ FTE searcher |
|---|---|---|---|
| Pennsylvania | .30 | 381 | 1270 |
| Pennsylvania State | 1.50 | 298 | 199 |
| Pittsburgh | 1.75 | 2087 | 1192 |
| Queen's | .25 | 295 | 1180 |
| Rice | .20 | 80 | 400 |
| Rutgers | .50 | 420 | 340 |
| Southern California | .10 | 188 | 1880 |
| Stanford | | 113 | |
| SUNY-Buffalo | 1.00 | 1200 | 1200 |
| SUNY-Stony Brook | 1.00 | 636 | 636 |
| Syracuse | | | |
| Temple | .50 | 661 | 1322 |
| Tennessee | 1.60 | 936 | 585 |
| Texas A & M | 3.00 | 2500 | 833 |
| Texas | 1.90 | 617 | 325 |
| Tulane | .10 | 241 | 2410 |
| Vanderbilt | .35 | 163 | 466 |
| Virginia | | 286 | |
| Washington | .75 | 865 | 1153 |
| Washington State | | 4257 | |
| Wisconsin | .75 | 685 | 913 |
| Yale | .25 | 21 | 84 |

Summary 4.  Online Fee Structures for Faculty and Students at

Institutions Surveyed

|  | N | % |
|---|---|---|
| Departments which recover full costs | 25[1] | 39 |
| Departments which recover full costs and add a service charge | 24[2] | 37 |
| Departments which charge a flat fee | 7[3] | 11 |
| Departments which subsidize searching | 8[4] | 12 |
| Departments which offer searching free | 1 | 1 |

[1]Two charge a $5.00 minimum.  One assesses a 17% service charge if the bill is paid in cash.

[2]Service charges are assessed either as a flat dollar amount, on an hourly bases or as a percentage of the total search cost.  Flat dollar amounts range from $1.00 to $12.00 with the average being $4.50.  Hourly charges range from $3.00/hour to $12.00/hour.  Percent charges range from 3% plus sales tax (where applicable) to 15%.  Of the 7 departments which assess a percent surcharge, 3 charge 10% and 3 charge 15%

[3]Flat fees charged by different libraries are as follows:  (1) $7.50 (to cover up to fifty citations and three databases); (2) $5.00 to $20.00 per database; (3) $2.00; (4) $30.00; (5) $10.00 for 20 minutes and thereafter 100 percent of cost; (6) either $5.00, $7,50 or $10.00, depending on the cost of the database; (7) fee based on average cost of search in the database plus offline printing and royalties; and (8) $2.50 for the first database entered and $1.25 for each additional database.

[4]Library subsidies are as follows:  (1) $2.00; (2) 50% of cost; (3) second $10.00 paid by the library; (4) 90% of all charges except print charges; (5) 20% of costs; (6) all BRS searching subsidized except for the cost of offline prints; and (7) all costs except on and offline printing.

Summary 5. Differential Online Searching Fee Structures in Use For Non-University Patrons.

| Institution | General Public | Non-Profit Organiz. | For-Profit Organiz. | Alumni |
|---|---|---|---|---|
| Arizona St. | $10 surcharge | $25 surcharge | $25 surcharge | $10 surcharge |
| Columbia | $50 surcharge | $50 surcharge | $50 surcharge | $25 surcharge |
| Florida | 9% surcharge | 6% surcharge | 9% surcharge | 9% surcharge |
| Indiana | $15 for the first database entered, $5 for each additional database | $5 for the first database entered, $2.50 for each additional database | $25 for the first database entered, $15 for each additional database or 50% of the cost (whichever is higher) $10 surcharge | same as the general public |
| Louisiana State | $25 surcharge | $10 surcharge | $10 surcharge | $10 surcharge |
| Massachusetts | treated the same as campus users | treated the same as campus users | $35 surcharge | treated the same as campus users (unless working for a for-profit organization) |
| Minnesota | treated the same as campus users | treated the same as campus users | $10 surcharge | treated the same as campus users |
| NYU | $35 surcharge | $35 surcharge | 35 surcharge | $25 surcharge |
| Notre Dame | $10 surcharge | $5 surcharge | $10 surcharge | treated the same as campus users |
| Pennsylvania | $10 surcharge | $10 surcharge | $30 surcharge | $10 surcharge |
| Temple | $10 surcharge | $10 surcharge | $25 surcharge | treated the same as campus users |
| Tennessee | $10 surcharge | $10 surcharge | $20 surcharge | " |
| Texas A & M | treated the same as other campus users | treated the same as other campus users | $10/hr surcharge | " |
| Washington State | " | " | unspecified service charge | " |

Table 11. Online Ready Reference and Verification Searching in Research
Library Reference Departments

| Institution | Ready-Reference and Verification Searches Done | | | |
| --- | --- | --- | --- | --- |
| | 1977/78 | 1978/79 | 1979/80 | 1980/81 |
| UC-Berkeley | ---- | ---- | 52 | 138 |
| UCLA | 6 | 9 | 39 | 33 |
| UC-San Diego | ---- | ---- | 157 | 204 |
| Chicago | ---- | 5 | 7 | 10 |
| Cornell | 131 | 290 | 289 | 381 |
| Delaware | ---- | ---- | ---- | 19 |
| Florida | 5 | 10 | 30 | 50 |
| Hawaii | ---- | ---- | ---- | 11 |
| Kentucky | ---- | 23 | 20 | 39 |
| Manitoba | ---- | 162 | 149 | ---- |
| Massachusetts | 86 | 117 | 131 | 168 |
| Michigan St. | ---- | ---- | 712 | 1076 |
| Pennsylvania | ---- | 133 | 270 | 342 |
| Stanford | ---- | ---- | 278 | 897 |
| Temple | ---- | 123 | 90 | ---- |
| Texas | ---- | ---- | 45 | 98 |
| Texas A & M | ---- | ---- | 200 | 2000 |
| Vanderbilt | ---- | ---- | ---- | 6 |
| Washington | ---- | ---- | ---- | 389 |
| Wisconsin | ---- | 40 | 92 | 87 |
| Average no. of Searches/year | 38.0 | 91.2 | 150.6 | 330.4 |
| Median no. of Searches/year | 5.5 | 40 | 92 | 118 |

Table 12.  Reference Departments' Budget and Collection Size.

| Institution | Budget | | | Volumes |
| --- | --- | --- | --- | --- |
| | Monographs | Serials | Total | in Collection |
| Alabama | 22,000 | | N.A. | 46,000 |
| Arizona | 25,000[2] | N.A.[1] | N.A. | |
| Arizona St. | N.A. | N.A.[3] | N.A. | 21,800 |
| Brigham Young | N.A.[4] | N.A.[1] | N.A. | N.A. |
| Brown | N.A. | N.A. | N.A. | 20,000 |
| Cal.-Berkeley | N.A. | N.A. | N.A. | N.A. |
| Cal.-Irvine | N.A. | N.A. | 25,000 | N.A. |
| UCLA | 15,000 | 25,000 | 40,000[5] | 40,000+ |
| Cal.-San Diego | N.A. | N.A. | N.A. | N.A. |
| Cal.-Santa B. | N.A. | N.A. | 80,000 | 30,000+ |
| Case Western | 2,000 | N.A.[1] | N.A. | 11,000+ |
| Chicago | 10,500 | 31,000 | 42,500 | 15,000-20,000 |
| Cincinnati | | | 7,000 | 27,000e |
| Colorado | 40,000 | N.A. | N.A. | 26,670 |
| Columbia | 20,000 | N.A.[1] | N.A. | 38,145 |
| Connecticut | 18,000 | N.A.[1] | N.A. | 34,000 |
| Cornell | N.A. | N.A. | 90,837 | 19,000 |
| Delaware | 16,000 | 36,000 | 52,000 | 25,000 |
| Duke | N.A. | N.A. | N.A. | 23,000e |
| Florida | 70,000 | 90,000 | 160,000 | 64,304 |
| Georgetown | N.A. | N.A. | N.A. | 18,500 |
| Georgia Tech. | N.A. | N.A. | N.A. | 42,000 |
| Harvard | N.A. | N.A. | N.A. | 5,000 |
| Hawaii | 22,000 | N.A. | N.A. | 20,000 |
| Houston | N.A. | N.A. | N.A. | N.A. |
| Illinois | 23,763 | 61,540 | 85,293 | 22,000 |
| Indiana | 29,753 | 46,947 | 76,700 | 28,000 |
| Iowa | 34,000 | 62,570 | 96,570 | 35,000 |
| Johns Hopkins | N.A. | N.A. | N.A. | N.A. |
| Kansas | 12,000 | varies | N.A. | 18,000 |
| Kentucky | 26,000 | 67,000 | 93,000 | 11,650 |
| Louisiana | 31,000 | N.A.[1] | N.A. | 21,318 |
| Manitoba | 8,244 | N.A.[1] | N.A. | 22,830 |
| Massachusetts | N.A.[3] | N.A.[3] | N.A.[3] | 18,000e |
| Michigan St. | N.A.[3] | N.A.[3] | N.A.[3] | 50,000 |
| Minnesota | N.A. | N.A. | N.A. | N.A. |
| Missouri | 33,530 | N.A.[1] | N.A. | 40,000 |
| New Mexico | 15,700 | 0[6] | --- | 20,000 |
| NYU | 20,000 | 24,624 | 44,624 | 21,600 |
| No. Carolina St. | N.A. | N.A. | N.A. | 25,000 |
| Northwestern | 35,500 | 66,000 | 101,500 | 47,700 |
| Notre Dame | 19,000 | 47,103 | 66,103 | 25,000 |
| Oklahoma | 11,500e | 45,000e | 56,500e | 18,000 |
| Oregon | 17,250 | 34,176 | 51,426 | 35,000 |
| Pennsylvania | N.A. | N.A. | N.A. | 30,000 |
| Pennsylvania St. | 20,000 | 84,000 | 104,000 | 23,421 |
| Pittsburgh | 17,029 | 37,500 | 54,529 | N.A. |

| Institution | Budget | | | Volumes |
| | Monographs | Serials | Total | in Collection |
| --- | --- | --- | --- | --- |
| Queen's | 25,000[7] | 25,000[7] | 50,000[7] | 15,300 |
| Rice | 12,505 | 133,614 | 146,119 | 10,356[8] |
| Rutgers | N.A.[3] | N.A.[3] | N.A.[3] | N.A. |
| Southern Cal. | 16,000 | 46,000 | 62,000 | 15,000e |
| Stanford | N.A. | N.A. | 92,054[9] | 37,138[10] |
| SUNY-Buffalo | 24,631 | 67,066 | 91,697 | 22,000 |
| SUNY-Stony Brook | 39,000 | 70,000 | 109,000 | 22,000 |
| Syracuse | 99,180 | 125,500 | 224,680 | 22,000e |
| Temple | 18,000e | N.A.[1] | N.A. | 20,000e |
| Tennessee | N.A.[3] | N.A.[3] | N.A.[3] | 17,000e |
| Texas A & M | 25,000[11] | 10,000[11] | 35,000[11] | 10,000 |
| Texas | 33,000[12] | 4,025[13] | 37,025 | 29,300 |
| Tulane | N.A. | N.A. | N.A. | 35,000 |
| Vanderbilt | 10,000 | 43,000 | 53,000 | 22,535[14] |
| Virginia | N.A. | N.A. | 18,000 | 27,152 |
| Washington | 18,848 | 5,185 | 24,033 | 26,126 |
| Washington St. | N.A. | N.A. | N.A. | 26,000e |
| Wisconsin | 86,612 | 47,940 | 134,552 | 77,888 |
| Yale | N.A.[3] | N.A.[3] | N.A.[3] | 34,000 |

[1] Serials budget not separately broken out for Reference.
[2] Base figure adjustable upward.
[3] Unallocated budget
[4] General Reference and Subject reference share a monograph budget of $25,000.
[5] Also have access to "Current Books" fund and a continuation fund to which around $10,000 is charged.
[6] No money for new serials; must cancel in order to add.
[7] Canadian
[8] Titles, not volumes
[9] FY84
[10] 1977 estimate
[11] New materials only
[12] Excludes approval plans
[13] New subscriptions only.
[14] As of 8/81

Table 13.  Staff Size Changes.

| | Librarians | | | Clerical Staff | | |
| | 1977/78 | 1983 | FTE Change | 1977/78 | 1983 | FTE Change |
|---|---|---|---|---|---|---|
| Alabama | | | | 2.00 | 3.00 | +1.00 |
| Arizona | 8.00 | 10.00 | +2.00 | 11.00 | 9.00 | −2.00 |
| Arizona State | 11.00 | 14.00 | +3.00 | 2.00 | 3.00 | +1.00 |
| BYU | 3.00 | 3.00 | none | 2.00 | 3.00 | +1.00 |
| Brown | 9.00 | 11.00 | +2.00 | 4.00 | 2.00 | −2.00 |
| UC-Irvine | 7.00 | 7.00 | none | 2.65 | 3.00 | + .35 |
| UCLA | 10.00 | 10.00 | none | 7.00 | 8.00 | +1.0 |
| UC-San D. | 9.00 | 9.95 | +0.95 | 2.00 | 2.00 | none |
| UC-Santa B. | 13.00 | 10.00 | −3.00 | 9.00 | 8.50 | − .50 |
| Chicago | 5.75 | 6.00 | + .25 | 1.00 | | |
| Cincinnati | 8.00 | 10.75 | +2.75 | | 6.00 | ? |
| Columbia | 6.00 | 6.00 | none | | 0 | |
| Connecticut | 7.00 | 8.00 | +1.00 | 3.00 | 1.0[1] | −2.00 |
| Cornell | 7.50 | 7.00 | −.50 | 2.00 | 3.50 | +1.50 |
| Delaware | 10.00 | 15.75 | +5.75 | 8.50 | 11.50 | +3.00 |
| Duke | | | none | | | |
| Florida | 15.00 | 14.50 | − .50 | 7.00 | 8.00 | +1.00 |
| Georgetown | 5.25 | 6.50 | +1.25 | 2.00 | 2.50 | + .50 |
| Ga. Tech. | 7.00 | 7.00 | none | 2.00 | 1.00 | −1.00 |
| Hawaii | 9.00 | 8.00 | −1.00 | 2.00 | 2.00 | none |
| Houston | ? 12.00 | 17.00 | +5.00 | ?18.00 | 22.50 | +4.5 |
| Illinois | 7.00 | 7.00 | none | 2.00 | 2.00 | none |
| Indiana | 6.00 | 6.00 | none | 5.75 | 4.00 | −1.75[2] |
| Kansas | 9.00 | 8.50 | + .50 | 1.00 | 1.00 | none |
| Kentucky | 7.00 | 6.00 | −1.00 | | 1.00 | +1.0? |
| Louisiana St. | 7.00 | 9.00 | +2.00 | 5.00 | 4.00 | −1.0 |

| | Librarians | | | Clerical Staff | | |
|---|---|---|---|---|---|---|
| | 1977/78 | 1983 | FTE Change | 1977/78 | 1983 | FTE Change |
| Manitoba | 9.00 | 11.35 | +2.35 | 7.00 | 10.00 | +3.0 |
| Massachusetts | 10.50 | 10.50 | none | 3.00 | 3.00 | none |
| Michigan St. | 10.50 | 12.00 | +1.5 | 1.50 | 1.50 | none |
| New Mexico | 13.00 | 13.00 | none | 4.00 | 4.00 | none |
| NYU | 7.50 | 8.00 | + .50 | 3.00 | | |
| No.Caro.St. | 6.00 | 6.00 | none | 4.00 | 4.00 | none |
| Notre Dame | 5.50 | 6.50 | +1.0 | 6.00 | 7.00 | +1.0 |
| Oklahoma | previously a divisional system | | | | | |
| Oregon | previously a divisional system | | | | | |
| Pennsylvania | 9.50 | 10.50 | +1.0 | | | |
| Penn St. | 10.75 | 10.50 | - .25 | 6.00 | 5.00 | -1.0 |
| Pittsburgh | 7.00 | 8.00 | +1.00 | 2.00 | 2.00 | none |
| Queen's | 6.00 | 4.66 | -1.34 | 4.00 | 4.00 | none |
| Rice | 3.00 | 6.00 | +3.00 | 0 | 0 | none |
| Rutgers | 5.00 | 8.00 | +3.00 | 1.00 | 2.00 | +1.0 |
| USC | 8.00 | 7.00 | -1.00 | 2.00 | 3.00 | +1.0 |
| Stanford | 6.00 | 5.00 | -1.00 | 12.50 | 8.00 | -4.5 |
| SUNY-Buff. | 6.00 | 6.30 | + .30 | 1.00 | 1.00 | none |
| SUNY-St.Br. | 13.00 | 13.75 | + .25 | 8.00 | 8.00 | none |
| Syracuse | 10.00 | 10.00 | none | 2.00 | 3.00 | +1.0 |
| Tennessee | 8.00 | 12.00 | +4.0[3] | | 3.00 | |
| Texas | 8.00 | 10.00 | +2.0 | 6.00 | 17.00 | +11.0 |
| Washington | 6.00 | 4.95 | -1.05 | 5.00 | 4.00 | -1.0 |
| Wisconsin | 5.00 | 5.00 | none | 2.50 | 3.50 | +1.0 |

1Apparently due to loss of interlibrary loan function.
2May be due to loss of interlibrary lending function.
3Science and Engineering Reference were combined with general reference in 1981.